Praise for *The Right Hire*

"If you've ever made a bad hire, regretted it, and wished you could be just a little more certain you wouldn't make the same expensive mistake all over again, Lisette Howlett's book is the answer to your dilemma."

—**ELIZABETH CLAYPOOLE,** Chief People Officer, AgBiome Inc., Triangle Park, North Carolina

"Talent is the ultimate resource. This book shows, accessibly and definitively, the best ways to secure it for your organisation."

—**ROGER PLAHAY,** Chief Financial Officer, Progresif Cellular SDN BHD, Bandar Seri Begawan, Brunei

"A definitive piece of work that will support successful leaders and HR professionals for years to come. Highly recommended."

—**JAMES CHESSUM,** Director, Red 5 Recruitment Solutions, London, UK

D1599395

SANDLER MANAGEMENT SERIES

THE RIGHT HIRE

Attract and Retain the Best People

Lisette Howlett

Foreword by DAVID MATTSON

To Peter

To Nicole

Contents

Acknowledgments

First and foremost, I would like to thank Peter, the love of my life, for his nurturing support throughout our lives together and for his help during the long period when I was writing and revising this book. I am grateful in particular for his willingness to check and re-check the entire manuscript for sense, grammar, and consistency. We may not have always agreed on the correct use of the semicolon, but we agreed on the importance of the project. Without Peter's help, there would have been a horrible mishmash throughout.

Thanks are also due to David Mattson, president and CEO of Sandler Training, and to the whole team at the home office who helped to move *The Right Hire* forward: Margaret Stevens Jacks, Rachel Miller, Jennifer Willard, Erica Stubbs, Yusuf Toropov, Jerry Dorris, and Laura Matthews. Without them, we would not have a published book. I would also like to take this opportunity to express my gratitude to the Sandler UK team, in particular to Fiona Thomson, who has been a wonderful advocate for this project.

Finally, I must thank the many colleagues and clients with whom I have worked over the years, who helped me to learn so much of what follows.

Foreword

Talent is the ultimate resource, and the resource most organizations are likeliest to mismanage.

In *The Right Hire,* Lisette Howlett shares a proven system for attracting the very best people to your organization. She also offers some important insights on holding onto those people once they're on your team. The best practices she shares—inspired by the work of David Sandler, the founder of our company—have been tested in multiple industries over a period of decades. Put simply: These strategies work.

These strategies may not be how you are used to attracting and retaining the best talent. They may require you to go outside your comfort zone, at least at first. But if you give them an honest try and implement them consistently, you will find out for yourself that they have the potential to transform your team—and your entire organization.

David Mattson
President/CEO, Sandler Training

Introduction

This book shares insights and best practices for hiring that have proven effective in a wide variety of industries. It is concerned with building capability in strategic recruitment, which in turn builds high-performing employees.

Hiring is a topic close to my heart because it goes to the core of the employment relationship. It is the start of the psychological bond that can make or break you as an employer. My own background lends itself to some unique insights that I hope you will enjoy, learn from, build on, and share.

In writing this book, I have used my experience of recruiting talent for many types of companies, for many types of jobs (from refuse collectors and front-line staff to salespeople and sales managers, senior executives and non-executive directors), and in several countries (indeed several continents), and melded this with my coaching experience (nine years as an award-winning Sandler® consultant and trainer) to produce this guide to recruitment that is informed by my human resources experience and the Sandler approach to sales.

Employee capability development (the foundation of the success of any organisation) encompasses strategic intent, people, processes, enabling tools and technology, management information, and culture. A good hiring process, it must be noted, also leads to better retention of talent. Using these concepts as my foundation, I have developed a simple model for hiring talent based on seven steps:

1. Strategy and context
2. Culture and attitude

3. Define and template
4. Prospect and attract
5. Qualify and select
6. Appoint and onboard
7. Measure and improve

Chapter 1 presents the model visually and provides a brief overview of each step. A more detailed and thorough discussion of each step is then provided in Chapters 2–8. Chapter 9 focuses on working with recruitment agencies. Chapter 10 explores recruitment evolution from transactional to strategic, and the Epilogue sums everything up.

Being able to attract, secure, and retain talent is a core competitive advantage. There are challenges to companies of any size, from small to very big. The challenges may manifest themselves differently, but at their simplest, they are concerned with finding, hiring, and keeping talent that will flourish in your organisation and enable you to meet your organisational ambitions.

Hiring is both an art and a science. The science part requires the development and consistent application of best practices, many of which can be found in this book. The art part is about learning and growing as a recruiter and as an organisation. Ideas and suggestions on this are also contained in this book.

You will see throughout the book references to selling and marketing because they both play a part in hiring. I have included a number of core business models that I have applied to the hiring arena to put hiring into a business context. The examples in this book mostly relate to hiring in the executive and sales arena in order to bring some focus to the book. The lessons, however, apply to other areas equally well.

This book does not focus on the legal side of recruitment, in the main because to cover recruitment-related legislation across the world would be a book in itself. This does not mean that this is not an important part of recruitment. It is important, and everything written here should be read in the context of the rule and spirit of the law within which you are operating. If you are to hire excellence, you need to ensure that you have a truly diverse workforce and, to this end, you must eradicate bias, both legal and illegal.

I very much believe that organisations and the people in them can be excellent. Excellence is more than mere financial success. Of course, organisations must be financially successful (within their chosen operating context); failure to succeed financially will render them unviable, and this serves no purpose. But they need to have a purpose greater than simple financial success—a purpose beyond profit. It is this purpose that will enable them to attract and retain the best talent.

The intent or desire to be excellent needs to be underpinned by the competency to be so. Thus, the desire to hire, retain, develop, and deploy the best talent with the right attitude needs to be underpinned by a willingness to invest the time, effort, and money required to develop the necessary hiring understanding and competence. This book seeks to make a contribution to the development of attitude, behaviour, understanding, and competence in all aspects of the intricately interconnected objectives of hiring and retention.

CHAPTER 1

The Hiring Process Model

Before exploring the elements of hiring in detail, it is important to understand the interactions between those elements and their interdependencies. To this end, this book includes a model for the hiring process, one that enables you to see everything at a glance and to navigate the steps of effective hiring within your organisation.

The diagram on the next page provides a model for hiring. Each element will be covered in more detail in the following chapters.

As can be seen from the model, all hiring needs to be in line with the overall strategy and context, underpinned by culture and attitude. The absence of either of these elements will result in costly hiring errors and loss of access to top talent.

Defining and templating is the kick-off piece to the hiring journey. It is separate to the elements of the funnel because this

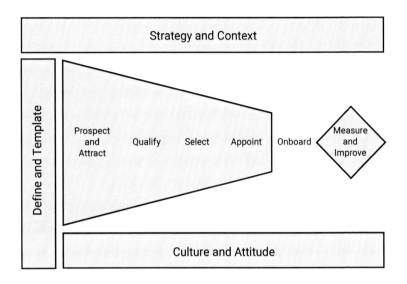

is something that can and should be done up front and used in organisation design as well as hiring. It is important to both employees and prospective employees.

The steps within the model (attract, qualify, select, appoint) are a funnel through which you take steps to reduce the numbers of candidates. This operates more on a campaign basis when you are selecting for particular roles within the organisation. Candidates who do not progress through the funnel for a particular role may be retained for future roles or released to pursue their careers elsewhere.

Onboarding is critical to both ultimate performance and speed to achieving that performance. It deserves more attention than it often receives. Too frequently, the hiring manager, exhausted by the effort required to find, attract, and secure top talent, ignores this step. However, onboarding increases the chances of that top talent achieving optimum performance as quickly as possible. A strong onboarding process also makes a significant contribution to retention.

The last step of the process is to measure and improve. This means making a commitment to evaluate and upgrade your hiring process over time.

Let's look more closely at each of these elements now.

Strategy and Context

Hiring must not be undertaken in a vacuum. While the ability to develop and consistently follow a hiring system is critical to success, both in terms of bringing new talent to the organisation and ensuring the ultimate success of the organisation, this is not sufficient. The strategy and context of each hire sets the framework for who and why you should be hiring. The cost of error here can be very high, so be strategic, be courageous, be systematic, and get it right.

Culture and Attitude

The culture and attitude element underpins the entire hiring process. This section examines the organisation's culture and attitude toward hiring; later sections will look at hiring for attitude, namely the attitude of the candidates and their cultural fit to the organisation. Congruence between the two is important. If you use one message with early stage candidates but their later recruitment experience undercuts that message, it will be the latter experience that will count. The ABC of hiring is "always be courting." This means to always focus on the candidate. This includes establishing a compelling, authentic, and congruent candidate value proposition. Another important aspect of culture and attitude is "always be recruiting" because of the importance of constantly being on the lookout for scarce talent and snapping it up wherever you find it.

Define and Template

This is the nuts and bolts of recruitment: defining the job, specifying the candidate, and templating the process. Getting this step right is critical to success but, as is so often true with planning and preparation, it can be overlooked, rushed, or done superficially. There is a strong similarity with sales meeting preparation and planning. Given how much effort, time, and money is invested in hiring new talent, it is disappointing when this element is skipped since this will negatively impact success. The SEARCH model, explored later, will elucidate this step.

Prospect and Attract

There are many parallels between selling and recruiting. As in sales, prospecting and pipeline management are both critical elements of successful recruitment. Recruitment (as with prospecting) needs to be a continuous, ongoing exercise. From time to time, a more specific campaign will be required, but to ensure the availability of top talent, a long-term approach needs to be adopted and your pipeline of potential talent needs to be nurtured and managed. Similarly, the more effective your forecasting of hiring requirements, the better you can plan for and meet business requirements. Adopting a multi-channel approach to attracting talent is critical to keeping your pipeline full. As with sales, the fuller the pipeline, the greater your choice.

Qualify and Select

This stage of the hiring process is where you qualify candidates using a range of different tools and techniques. The elements include inventorying, screening, interviewing, and evaluating. Inventorying is looking at what you have. Screening focuses on reducing the number of potential candidates to a manageable size for selection. Evaluating is about matching them to your pre-defined requirements. Interviewing, while not an exact science, also plays a key part here. The better trained your interviewer, the better chance of success in identifying the match between candidate and the role. Using effective interview techniques, such as behavioural interviewing reinforced by the right assessments, will also increase your success rate and your rate of retention. Relying on subjective assessments of "chemistry" may, at best, result in an organisation filled with people just like you—but will also leave you missing out on top talent.

Appoint and Onboard

This step includes the assessment and decision-making steps set in the strategic context. Deciding on the candidate you want is, of course, the first part; next, you have to ensure that they decide that they want to join your organisation. In traditional sales, this step is the close, and, as any trained salesperson knows, the close happens earlier in the process than most people think. This is exactly the same for hiring. Successful closing occurs during the selection process—when the candidate starts to think, "This is the company I want to work for"—and not when an offer is made. Indeed, if you have not closed during the process, the offer step will become protracted with a high risk that the candidate will not accept.

The onboarding steps are the second most overlooked element of hiring, yet they are critical to the overall success of the hire. Poor onboarding can lead to a slow (and costly) time to effectiveness and ultimately make all the difference between a candidate staying and succeeding or failing and leaving. Compensation also plays a part in the successful attraction, retention, and performance of your new hire. It is an area where it pays to think it through care-fully up front; once offered, elements of a compensation package are very hard to change.

Measure and Improve

Alas, the measuring, learning, and improving step is the most neglected part of hiring. When it is done, it usually only focuses on the short-term hiring process alone—how the process ran rather than how the hire worked out. In this hiring system, this step is all about evaluating and improving both (one of the benefits of having a system and template). This step also focuses on the firm's hiring competence: how effective and how efficient managers are at hiring and what the quality is of hires in the mid- to long-term. It allows you to evaluate how effective you are at predicting high performance and high potential when you hire.

Chapter Summary

The elements of the hiring process, as described by the hiring process model:

1. Strategy and context
2. Culture and attitude
3. Define and template
4. Prospect and attract
5. Qualify and select
6. Appoint and onboard
7. Measure and improve

Chapters 2–8 will go into more depth on each of the elements of the model, challenging assumptions and sharing best practices as well as giving tools and techniques.

CHAPTER 2

Strategy and Context

This chapter explores the strategy and context of hiring. Taking context first, I have included an in-depth exploration of the cost of error in hiring, covering direct, indirect, and opportunity costs. This kind of analysis enables hiring professionals to support their case for investments of time and attention to the hiring process at both the organisational and individual level.

At the organisational level this means investing in strong hiring processes, upskilling managers involved in hiring, and expending the effort required to take a holistic and long-term approach to hiring. At the individual level, this means making time in busy schedules to hire well and developing the foresight, confidence, and courage to hire strategically despite the often overwhelming short-term pressures to just get the vacancy filled.

I have also sought to put the issue of recruitment into a broader business and people context, sharing some approaches and insights that I believe will support a more balanced view of recruitment and hiring than is often taken. This means thinking of recruitment as talent management, an approach that is new to many managers.

Cost of Error

Have you ever found yourself thinking, "This person is not quite what I hoped for, but we are really shorthanded so they will have to do," when recruiting? It is tempting. Many times when looking to hire a new team member, you are at your busiest as you strive to cover the vacancy, and this adds to the pressure.

Or, have you ever put up with a poor or mediocre hire just because you haven't the time or bandwidth to tackle their dismissal followed by a lengthy search? It's not unusual.

If you have ever done either, then have a good look at the cost. This might convince you to never do this again.

To set the scene, let's first consider the cost of hiring mistakes.

Industry estimates put the cost of a bad hire at somewhere between 1 and 2.5 times the person's annual salary. For salespeople, the true cost is, in fact, considerably higher when you build in opportunity costs. Our estimate, based on experience, is that this falls somewhere between 10 and 25 times the annual salary. The cost of a bad hire for salespeople is worrying; the cost of a bad hire for senior executives is almost incalculable. You are putting at risk the future of the organisation and its growth, shareholder value, and reputation. Also, it is harder to measure. You might not even know the cost of the damage of a poor senior executive hire since you will not know what you might have achieved with a strong hire.

Before exploring cost elements, it's important to differentiate between a "bad hire" (one that you spot and deal with in a timely manner) and a "poor or mediocre hire" (one that you tolerate within the organisation for many years to come). Interestingly, it is the poor or mediocre hires that cost the organisation the most, and yet they are the most difficult to mobilise management to deal with. Certainly, I know from my days in HR that tolerance of mediocrity was a costly and damaging phenomenon among some managers. There are a number of reasons for this: managers are very busy; it is an important but not urgent activity so it slips to the bottom of the priority list; nobody likes to give bad messages; people become integrated into the organisation and managers worry about the impact of removal; the philosophy of "the one you know is better than the one you don't"; the list goes on. A significant part of this is the sense of dread and exhaustion many managers feel about having first to cover the resulting vacancy and second to hire the replacement. In some organisations, fear that the replacement hire will not be sanctioned due to cost-saving measures or hiring freezes can be a major stumbling block as well.

I developed a few tricks to address this issue.

- Reward managers who tackle mediocrity with a guarantee that they will be allowed to replace underperforming employees with a stronger, more suitable candidate. This is particularly important when the organisation is under cost pressure. Managers fear that if they fire a team member they will not be able to replace the person, and thus cling to mediocre staff on the basis that someone is better than nobody.
- Help managers work out the lifetime cost of continuing to employ the mediocre employee. Just stick to direct costs: salary and overheads. Don't worry about opportunity

costs, lack of productivity, lack of creativity, etc. When working out this number, it is safe to assume that this person will not voluntarily leave and will therefore be with the organisation for many years to come. Using 25 years and an average salary of £30,000+ (let's be conservative) and a 30% overhead, and you easily get close to £1,000,000. Ask the manager (or yourself) if you would prefer to invest £1,000,000 in this individual or someone new. You might be pleased with the answer.

You can work out your own costs of a potential hiring mistake using the checklist below. Costs can be broken down into six broad categories:

- The cost of hiring the person
- The direct compensation costs
- The cost of employing the person
- The cost of exiting the person
- Opportunity costs
- Impact or disruption costs

Let's look at each one in turn.

Hiring Costs

The hiring costs should be fairly transparent. If they are not currently being tracked, you should start tracking them now. These are the direct and indirect costs involved in hiring the individual.

Generally, I would recommend that you look at the variable costs only when evaluating the cost of hiring mistakes—i.e., those costs that can be directly attributed to that individual hire—rather than seek to allocate overhead costs (hiring portal, recruitment fairs, etc.). If you do wish to allocate overhead, this can be calculated by dividing it by the number of successful hires per year. It is an important metric to track, but not in the context of cost of error since you will be hiring a replacement and thus can allocate the overhead to that replacement. When calculating the cost per hire overhead, you should take care to use successful hires as the denominator. If you divide the overall hiring overhead costs by the sum of both successful and unsuccessful hires, you will artificially lower the overhead/hire number and be tracking an incorrectly too-low number.

The variable costs you should track are:

- **Direct search fees or recruitment fees paid to an external agency.** Generally, these are paid as a percentage of total compensation (see Chapter 9 for more information) and typically range from 8% to 33% of base plus bonus (and possibly benefits). Most recruitment agencies have a rebate period, namely a period of time in which, if the candidate leaves, you either get a percentage of the fees refunded or a "free of charge" replacement. Take care when signing such agreements that this is not limited to the circumstance of the individual leaving rather than if you exit them. As you might imagine, recruitment agencies seek to keep these rebate periods as short as possible, which is further incentive to have a good onboarding approach and the ability to make a quick but accurate assessment of your new hire. If you have made a mistake, you need to realise it early and take immediate action.

- **Costs for any external assessments, interviewing, reference checking, medical review, etc.** Ignore the time taken if any of these activities are undertaken in-house. While these costs may not be overly high, they are not necessarily insignificant and should be monitored. As an aside, assessments are covered in more detail under inventorying in Chapter 6, but when selected correctly and used well, they can save an enormous amount of time (and cost) as well as increase your chance of making a strong hire.

- **Travel and related costs for the candidate and the recruiting team, hiring rooms for interview, bringing the family over to look around the area, and so on.** These costs can quickly mount up. If they are high, you might want to explore ways of reducing recruitment-related travel with better use of technology such as telephone and video interviewing, especially at the early stage of the process.

- **Relocation costs.** Depending on your company policy, this can add a very significant amount if you are hiring from outside the area and moving people. It also adds to the disinclination to exit the individuals quickly since managers feel, not unreasonably, somewhat responsible for the disruption to the employees and their family/dependents. I would recommend that you do not relocate someone and their family during a trial or probation period.

- **HR department time and administrative costs.** While at face value this may appear more of a fixed than variable cost, the time spent handling the particular individual's recruitment should be tracked and monitored. This is not just to help you calculate cost of hires but also to provide information to enable you to continuously improve your recruitment processes. If you have the data, you might simply use the average costs. Otherwise, you should do a calculation that allows for time to prepare for and conduct the interview, administer the candidate, make contact, book them in, do the joining paperwork, put them in your systems, etc.

- **Hiring manager and hiring team time and administrative**

costs. While there is an argument that there are opportunity costs involved here, generally it is sufficient to look at the actual time spent on hiring that individual (preparing and reading paperwork, interviewing, meeting, attending presentations, etc.). If you limit your analysis to direct costs (time spent times salary of the individuals), you should still bear in mind the indirect costs: less focus on goals; delays to project completion; opportunity costs (i.e., what they could have achieved had they not been spending time on recruitment). One of the reasons for not focusing on opportunity costs for the hiring team is that most often the team will make up the time by working longer hours and thus reduce impact (although there could be a reduction in quality). This, however, flags a wellbeing cost, which is the additional stress and pressure placed on the hiring team. In addition to team members' own roles, they have to find time to hire and also most probably to cover the work of the vacancy. The latter, ironically, is one of the main drivers for compromising when hiring (and thus making hiring mistakes)—the desire to get the role filled and lack of energy (mental as much as physical) to turn down a possibly OK candidate and start the process again.

Compensation Costs

This is fairly straightforward to calculate. You should include:

- Base salary.
- Bonus paid or payable upon exit. Include in here any signing bonus, performance bonus, guarantee bonus payments, etc.
- Stock options or stock issued that would vest on leaving.

- Benefits (medical, cars, pension, savings, membership, subscriptions).
- Other compensation that you have paid or are committed to paying.

The Cost of Employing the Person

Here you should include the overhead costs associated with onboarding and employing the individual. You should include the following:

- **Onboarding costs.** The costs and time associated with the formal onboarding programme. This would include health and safety briefings, meetings with executives (the time they spent with the new hire), on-the-job training time by colleagues, and management onboarding sessions and coaching (but exclude training costs, which are below).
- **Management costs.** This is the time taken to manage the new hires during their period of employment. Focus on one-to-one time rather than team time.
- **Training costs.** External costs incur a direct cost, which is easy to determine. Internal courses should also be counted since the new hires will have taken up a space and their replacements will need to be trained again.
- **Administrative assistant or sales support costs.** These are the costs associated with providing services during the period of employment. For salespeople, you might want to include any dedicated lead generation support as well.
- **Overhead costs.** This might include office rental, provision of furniture, computers, phones, and so on.
- **Any other employment or maintaining costs.**

The Cost of Exiting the Person

There are always costs to exiting an employee. When the situation is well-managed, the costs could be fairly low, but even well-managed exits may include payments that were put in place at the hiring stage to encourage them to join or indeed encourage them to not leave. Typically, costs may occur in the following areas:

- **Severance payment.** Depending on the length of service, the contract environment, and your organisation's policies and practices, there may be a direct payment that you are obliged or seek to make to the individual.

- **Outplacement support.** It may or may not be appropriate to pay for some level of outplacement support. This will vary depending on levels of seniority, length of service, and company practice.

- **Severance costs.** This will include payments in lieu of notice, holiday time not taken, and lawyers' fees (potentially both yours and theirs).

- **Losses.** These include costs of defending or settling any legal claims made, bad press, loss of clients, and reputational damage. Frequently the need to mitigate these is what leads to a severance payment that includes a confidentiality agreement.

- **Administrative costs.** These include HR and line management time spent planning, managing, and communicating the exit.

Opportunity Costs

Opportunity costs of missed or wasted business opportunities can be very significant indeed. For some jobs, they are much higher than others. Senior executive roles carry the highest opportunity costs and are the hardest to calculate. Sales and account management jobs are associated with some of the highest opportunity costs after senior executives. When we talk about opportunity costs in the employee context, we mean the cost of the missed or lost opportunities associated with poor (or mediocre) performance. You can explore the idea of opportunity costs further by looking at two examples, one for a CEO and one for a sales or account manager.

For senior roles, you are looking to compare actual business performance with that which might theoretically have been achieved by a stronger performer. This is clearly challenging since there are a number of other factors that can impact business performance and you do not have an alternative employee carrying out the same role. Nevertheless, it needs to be attempted. The following alternatives are available:

1. **Actual performance against budget.** As you would do with shareholders, explanations for the difference can be included (market conditions, etc.), but the gap needs to be identified. This comparison is particularly relevant to the CEO where there is individual accountability or for business unit heads with separate P&Ls.

2. **Performance against competitors.** This good way of benchmarking effectively takes into account prevailing market conditions since the employee will be facing them as well. Putting this into a longer timeframe can help, so look at historical performance against competitors along with the period under review. Thus, if in the past three years you have outperformed competitors by 12% and this year you outperform by 3%, this is a poor result. Without the historical comparison, outperforming by 3% might look positive.

3. **Performance against the previous years.** This is looking to see if the business growth trends are continuing.

4. **Public metrics.** Where the company is listed, you can track share price, analyst reports, etc.

5. **Cost of delays to entering new markets or launching new products.** Here you can calculate actual performance against forecast when putting the business case together for the launch.

6. **Internal metrics.** These include metrics around staff performance and motivation (survey reports if you do 360-degree feedback, or annual staff engagement question-naires), productivity, absence, and turnover levels (which provide a good indicator of leadership competence).

There are four alternative ways to calculate opportunity costs for salespeople where you have more than one employee in the same role. You can select the one that best fits your circumstances and the data available.

1. **Compare the value of sales of the individual to the value of a high-performing employee doing the same job.** As a rule of thumb (but you will want to use your own metrics), salespeople should bring in revenue that is at least 10 times their compensation. So a salesperson on a base compen-sation of £30,000 should be selling £300,000. This can, of course, be much higher. To illustrate this, using these numbers, if during the six months of employment this indi-vidual generated £10,000 in revenue, the opportunity cost you would record would be £140,000 in "missing" revenue.

2. **Compare the individual's closing performance against a high-performing colleague.** The benefit of doing this is that it also gives you an indication of lost revenue. If a

high-performing colleague closes one in three qualified leads and this individual closes one in six, you are effectively destroying the value of your pipeline. You will be leaving one client "on the table" each time. Taking your average client value into account allows you to calculate the cost of this.

3. **Calculate the cost of delays to entering new markets or launching new products.** Here you can calculate actual performance against forecast when putting the business case together for the launch. This is similar to #5 above but would only apply to new markets or products into which the individual is seeking to enter or sell.

4. **Calculate the cost of discounting.** Typically, the weaker the salesperson, the greater the discounting. Discounting takes money straight off your bottom line. Look at the table on the next page to see just how much—it may frighten you. Let's say your present margin is 20%; if you discount by 10%, you need to increase your sales by 100% to keep the same gross profit. The table showing the impact of price increases will enable you to calculate the added value of a high-performing salesperson who maintains higher prices.

Discounting Your Prices									
If your present margin is:	20%	25%	30%	35%	40%	45%	50%	55%	60%
and you discount your price by:	...your sales must increase by the amount shown to keep the same gross profit:								
2%	11%	9%	7%	6%	5%	5%	4%	4%	3%
4%	25%	19%	15%	13%	11%	10%	9%	8%	7%
6%	43%	32%	25%	21%	18%	15%	14%	12%	11%
8%	67%	47%	36%	30%	25%	22%	19%	17%	15%
10%	100%	67%	50%	40%	33%	29%	25%	22%	20%
12%	150%	92%	67%	52%	43%	36%	32%	28%	25%
14%	233%	127%	88%	67%	54%	45%	39%	34%	30%
16%	400%	178%	114%	84%	67%	55%	47%	41%	36%
18%	900%	247%	150%	106%	82%	67%	56%	49%	43%
20%	–	400%	200%	133%	100%	80%	67%	57%	50%
25%	–	–	500%	250%	167%	125%	100%	83%	71%
30%	–	–	–	600%	300%	200%	150%	120%	100%

The table shows the increase in sales required to compensate for a price discount. For example, if your margin is 40% and you reduce your price by 10%, you need your sales volume to increase by 33% to maintain your profit. Salespeople who discount typically cost the company money since they rarely compensate with increased sales volumes of the magnitude required.

Below, I have included a table showing the impact of price increases as well. This will enable you to calculate the added value of a high-performing salesperson who maintains higher prices.

Increasing Your Prices									
If your present margin is:	20%	25%	30%	35%	40%	45%	50%	55%	60%
and you increase your price by:	...your sales could decline by the amount shown to keep the same gross profit:								
2%	9%	7%	6%	5%	5%	4%	4%	4%	3%
4%	17%	14%	12%	10%	9%	8%	7%	7%	6%
6%	23%	19%	17%	15%	13%	12%	11%	10%	9%
8%	29%	24%	21%	19%	17%	15%	14%	13%	12%
10%	33%	29%	25%	22%	20%	18%	17%	15%	14%
12%	38%	32%	29%	26%	23%	21%	19%	18%	17%
14%	41%	36%	32%	29%	26%	24%	22%	20%	19%
16%	44%	39%	35%	31%	29%	26%	24%	23%	21%
18%	47%	42%	38%	34%	31%	29%	26%	25%	23%
20%	50%	44%	40%	36%	33%	31%	29%	27%	25%
25%	56%	50%	45%	42%	38%	36%	33%	31%	29%
30%	60%	55%	50%	46%	43%	40%	38%	35%	33%

The table above shows the amount by which your sales would have to decline following a price increase before your gross profit is reduced. Clearly if you maintain your sales, you will increase your gross profit. For example, if your margin is 40% and you increase your price by 10%, you could sustain a 20% reduction in sales volume. Interestingly, salespeople who maintain price and do not discount often sell more, which increases their contribution substantially. Thus, the gap between a top salesperson (or an A-Player) and an average one is quite significant.

Impact or Disruption Costs

Impact or disruption costs should be looked at in two ways: first, the impact the individual has on the organisation and your customers or clients; and second, the impact that employing this individual has on other employees. Let's look at the areas this may occur.

Impact on organisation and customers/clients

You may see cost in the areas of mistakes or failures caused by the individual's poor performance, lack of competence, or unacceptable attitude. When calculating the costs for these, include time and costs incurred to remedy the situation. Focus on the costs to the organisation.

There are also costs associated with a salesperson selling easy but low-margin products or solutions or selling to off-target clients or geographies. Lost value is taken into account under the missed opportunity calculation, but here you should also look at the detrimental impact on the organisation of increased complexity, having to service a higher numbers of clients, or unprofitable deals.

There will be direct and indirect (goodwill, reputation, etc.) costs associated with any damage caused to client or customer relationships. This could be due to the individual's inability to communicate or work effectively with clients, or it could be due to over-promising or misleading during the sale or client account management.

Customer service or the accounts management team will often bear the brunt of poor performance by the salesperson. They will be the ones dealing with clients who are unhappy because of delays (lost paperwork, poor follow through), being over-promised, or being pressured to buy something they did not fully understand (so they have unrealistic expectations of the product or service). Ideally your team will be well-trained and able to handle these issues without damaging the relationship with the client or your reputation in the market, but your team will feel the pressure nonetheless.

Another potential impact of poor performance on the sales, account management, or customer service areas is loss of referrals. To calculate the cost of this, consider the lifetime value of a client and the potential number of referrals a high-performing colleague would secure and close in a year compared to a poorly performing one. A simple lifetime value estimate would be to take your average annual spend multiplied by the average number of years you keep a client. For example, if the average annual spend of a client is £50,000 and the average retention rate is three years, you would get £150,000. Add to this the number of referrals and introductions you get each year for each client. For this illustration, let's be conservative and say you convert one introduction per year. This average client would therefore net you another three clients during the average customer lifetime. This adds another £450,000, bringing you to a lifetime value figure of £600,000. If you look at the referrals from the new clients, the number gets bigger and bigger—or smaller and smaller if your clients are sold to badly.

Impact on colleagues and employees

To estimate this cost of poor hires, you need to consider the cost of impaired teamwork and collaboration with the team. This can become an issue if an individual's performance is seen as impacting team rewards, time, or recognition of colleagues.

Similarly, poor performers can damage the productivity of the people they work and collaborate with within the organisation, either because others have to spend time helping the poor performer or fixing issues or because they are quite frankly fed up.

The degree of difficulty in firing someone increases in direct proportion to the amount of time that individual has been in the job.

While less quantifiable, the impact of individual morale cannot be overestimated. Colleagues will feel that they need to or find that they are required to cover the work of the poor performer. If you do not take action and a poor or mediocre employee is allowed to remain on the team, other team members may start to believe that high performance is not valued. In addition to negatively impacting motivation and productivity, this can lead to your high performers leaving for companies that they believe will value and reward them more. Morale can also be impacted by taking action. If you make a hiring error, the best solution is to act quickly and exit the individual. However, if you do this too often, you run the risk of inadvertently creating a hire-and-fire culture (or the belief that there is one), which will damage the morale and motivation of current employees.

Management time and attention is frequently spent on poor performers at the expense of high performers. Not only does this impact motivation and morale, but it also means that managers are not spending time coaching and encouraging high performers to achieve even more. This will have a significant impact on long-term growth and performance. Time invested in high performers will often give a much higher return than time wasted on poor performers, yet more time is allocated to managing poor performance than high performance.

Checklist for Calculating the Cost of a Hiring Error

Hiring costs

☐ Direct search fees or recruitment fees paid to an external agency.

☐ Costs for any external assessments, interviewing, reference checking, medical review, etc.

☐ Travel and related costs.

☐ Relocation costs.

☐ HR department time and administrative costs.

☐ Recruiting manager and recruiting team time and administrative costs.

Compensation costs

☐ Base salary.

☐ Bonus paid or payable upon exit. Include here any signing bonus, performance bonus, guaranteed bonus payments, etc.

☐ Stock options or stock issued that would be vested upon leaving.

☐ Benefits (medical, cars, pension, savings, membership, subscriptions).

☐ Other compensation that you have paid or are committed to paying.

The cost of employing the person

☐ Onboarding costs.

☐ Management costs.

☐ Training courses.

☐ Administrative or sales support provided during the period of employment.

☐ Overhead costs.

☐ Any other employment or maintaining costs.

The cost of exiting the person

☐ Severance payment.

☐ Outplacement support.

☐ Severance costs.

☐ Losses—cost of defending or settling any legal claims made, bad press, loss of clients, reputational damage, etc.

☐ Administrative costs.

Opportunity costs (cost of missed or wasted business opportunities)

☐ Difference in the value of sales of the individual and comparing to the value of a high-performing employee doing the same job.

☐ Difference in closing performance against a high-performing colleague.

☐ Cost of discounting.

☐ Cost of delays to entering new markets or launching new products.

Impact or disruption costs

☐ Cost of mistakes or failures.

☐ Cost of selling easy but low-margin products or solutions, or selling to off-target clients or geographies.

☐ Damage to customer relations.

☐ Loss of referrals.

☐ Impaired teamwork.

☐ Lower team productivity.
☐ The impact on team/individual morale.
☐ Management time and attention.

Do Something Today

✓ Do a quick back-of-the-envelope calculation of the costs of hiring the wrong salesperson. What did you learn?
✓ Now do a quick back-of-the-envelope calculation of the costs of hiring the wrong person in another position. What did you learn?

This section has provided a comprehensive overview of the costs of a bad hire. The table below offers a shortcut calculation that will underestimate the cost of a poor hire but will still make apparent just how costly a mistake it can be.

Quick Estimate: Costs of a Poor Hire	
1. Number of salespeople	
2. Number of salespeople hired each year averaged over the last three years	
3. Number of salespeople fired or resigned each year averaged over the last three years	
4. Average annual salary per salesperson	
5. Average annual revenue per salesperson	
6. Number of weeks it takes to replace a salesperson	
7. Recruiting/hiring costs per hire	
a. Advertising	
b. Agency fees	
c. Cost of management time	
d. Cost of HR support	
e. Admin costs	
8. Training and development costs per hire	
9. Number of weeks before salesperson is effective	

A = Turnover	#3 divided by #1 x 100
B = Weekly opportunity costs	#5 divided by 44 (52 minus holidays)
C = Onboarding costs	(#9 x B) + (#9 x #4 divided by 52)
D = Lost productivity costs	(#6 x B)

Total cost of a single bad hire = #7 + #8 + C + D	
Average cost of bad hires per year = (#7 + #8 + C + D) x #3	

Be Strategic

Finding and keeping top talent comes from first determining what top-talent candidates look like in your organisation—both now and in the future—and then working out how to best develop, inspire, and keep them.

A recruiter in the personnel world is like the archetypal salesperson in the commercial world. "Direct cost plus £0.01" is a worthwhile sale to this salesperson; this is the same as "find a candidate who meets the specifications" to the recruiter. But the commercially astute will respond to that salesperson with questions about opportunity costs, complexity, indirect costs, eroding value, etc. The same is true on the recruitment side.

The lack of strategic thinking in the recruitment area leads to similar problems—a weak pipeline, opportunity costs, business stagnation, high and often unquantifiable indirect costs, eroding organisation value, and so on.

> Strategy: A long-term plan of action designed to achieve a particular goal, most often "winning."
>
> Winning in this context is the ability to attract and retain the best talent for your organisation. This is best achieved by having a plan of action and thinking about the long term.
>
> Key elements are:
>
> - Think about the short and long term.
> - Have a plan and execute it rigorously.
> - Act strategically, not reactively.

Many see filling a vacancy as a chore at a time when they have the least time available. But to reframe it, recruiting is the best opportunity you have to move your organisation one step closer to your new vision; thus, the need is for a talent strategy (find, develop, and keep) that is aligned to the organisation vision and strategy.

When developing the strategy, you need to think about things at both the organisational and individual levels. What organisational capability will be required in three to five years for continued business success and the realisation of the new vision? This can be fundamental competencies (such as adaptability, change orientation, or dealing with ambiguity), and it can be broad numbers and skills, including locations/geography. Once you have determined that, move to the more granular. Think about what this means in terms of the people you need to recruit, the skills they need to acquire, and the development you need to support—and whether this means certain roles and skills will no longer be required.

My coaching colleagues and I have helped organisations ranging from five people to 25,000 people develop these strategies. While the complexity clearly varies, the fundamental elements are the same: what you have now, what you need more of, what you need less of, how to grow what you need, and how you buy what you can't develop.

Your recruitment strategy needs to focus on seven elements:

1. Filling positions through a blend of internal promotions and external recruitment.
2. Recruiting experienced top performers into key roles necessary for the future growth and success of the business.
3. Recruiting high potential team members into entry

roles so you can develop them to fill future roles within the business.

4. Identifying key strategic roles that you hire "to plan" rather than against vacancies; thus, you have a pre-need external search ongoing at all times.

5. Developing a branding and employee value proposition. This should have a compelling employment proposition and establish your brand as an employer of choice in your chosen markets (or aspirations and a plan to become one).

6. Developing a culture of recruitment in which employees are ambassadors and talent-spotters for the company.

7. Selecting candidates primarily through interviews, supplemented by psychometrics that screen candidates for pre-defined skills, behaviours, competencies, and attitudes.

Recruitment Framework

Adopting a more strategic approach to recruitment means viewing it not as a narrowly designed transaction but putting it into the wider context of your business and your people.

Recruitment is defined as everything you need to do to ensure that your organisation has the right number of people with the right skills to meet its current and future (frequently unknown) demand.

This requires recruitment to be placed in a much broader framework, i.e., that of talent management. Its goal is to ensure that you are able to fill a position at the time that you need it with the right person within a reasonable timeframe. It covers the following:

- **Resource planning.** Looking at demand and supply over time, being able to predict the skills, experiences, and capabilities you will need over the next twelve months, three years, and five years. If you have recruitment authorisation processes in operation, how well do you incorporate strategic goals and new capability requirements into them? If you are just checking that the budget is in place and there is nobody about to be made redundant who could do the job, you are missing a significant business opportunity.

- **Resourcing strategy.** Where and how you plan to attract candidates, develop talent pools, and invest in mid- to long-term approaches to access talent when you need it.

- **Job design and capability development.** Enabling you to fill jobs from within, identifying entry roles that you recruit and career paths into which you develop people, and being able to keep high performers motivated and challenged in their roles.

- **Selection.** The process of matching candidates to the organisation and role, and measuring and improving selection capability.

- **Appointment.** The process of making and closing the offer, ensuring a strong employee value proposition, and flexing the offer to suit individuals.

- **Retention.** Keeping high performers in the company and performing, encouraging the departure of mediocre performers, and swiftly exiting poor performers.

- **Management development.** Developing leadership capability, increasing commercial understanding, preparing leaders of the future, and increasing capability in change leadership, visioning, and communication.

- **Engagement.** Ensuring that staff understand and support the vision, value, strategy, and purpose, measuring and improving talent and skills, and ensuring that everyone is working toward the same overall goal.

- **Organisation design.** Maintaining a dynamic, responsive organisational structure and flexing the organisation to create development opportunities for individuals. When was the last time you used a vacancy to change the organisational structure, create development opportunities, and recruit someone quite different?

The core elements of the recruitment framework are:

- A well-defined strategy.
- Compelling and authentic employment branding.
- Efficient, effective, and creative sourcing.
- Strong selection competence.
- An embedded recruiting culture.
- A candidate-centric attitude.
- An integrated, strategic approach.
- Underpinned by technology.
- Measurement.

Do Something Today

✓ If you have a recruitment authorisation process, change this to incorporate fit with strategic goals and new capability requirements. Ask the question: What will filling this role do to take the organisation forward?

Be Courageous

Courage is the winning touch in recruitment and makes the difference between mediocrity or "just about OK" and excellence or A-talent.

The act of recruitment is an act of hope—you and the candidate both hope that this is the right move. Courage is not about making wildly inappropriate hires. This would not be fair to the company nor the individual. It is the ability to make a decision in the absence of perfect information and the confidence to see it through to success. If you decide to hire a candidate who has all

> Have you ever lost your nerve over a risky hire? Have you ever delayed the recruitment process to get more information only to lose the candidate to a competitor?
> Courage is not:
>
> - Making wildly inappropriate hires.
>
> Courage is:
>
> - Being willing to hire someone who is different than you and possibly with even higher potential.
> - Being able to make a decision in the absence of perfect information and the confidence to see it through to success.
> - Continuing to stick with your conviction and saying "no" even when other people are pushing a candidate.
> - Searching until the right candidate is found.

the right attributes but is short on experience, you need to ensure that the support, coaching, and development systems are in place; equally, if you hire people who are a bit different than the norm (such as risk takers in a more reserved culture), make sure they will not get so stifled that the very attribute you hired them for gets lost or they give up the fight and leave.

Let's consider the example of CEO Helena. Helena is the kind of person who does everything by her gut. She surrounds herself with capable people (she would be a fool not to) but when it comes to hiring decisions, she trusts her gut at the expense of all else. Helena therefore ensures she has the final say on all hires at the management and executive level. She lets her people follow their best-in-class hiring approach but asks that she has 20 minutes with their three best candidates. Then she chooses.

A few years back when she introduced this policy, she often found herself rejecting all the candidates. She was sure they did not have "what it takes." These days she always finds one she can hire. Reflecting on this progress, she prides herself on how fast her managers have learned. However, the question to ask is: What have her managers learned? Have they learned to find the top talent that Helena thinks only her gut can spot, or have they learned to only put forward people who fit Helena's preferences? If this over-reliance on Helena's preferences/gut is not addressed, it could result in any of the following:

- Departure of the existing management team.
- Gradual reduction in capability within the organisation.
- Lost opportunities to hire top talent.
- Litigation and diversity claims.

Thus, in this example, courage would be approaching Helena

and persuading her that her gut is not the best recruitment tool available.

Care needs to be taken not to confuse courage with poor management or autocratic leadership. Courage is not permission to hire based on the gut regardless of what the data is saying. Apart from the obvious risks of litigation and error, at best unstructured, unsystematic hiring will deliver you a team of weaker versions of yourself with all of your failings but fewer of your strengths. This is hardly ideal. Non-threatening, yes; ideal, no.

Your gut is perhaps better used to ensuring a more thorough discussion than to hire or reject a candidate. If it does not feel right, explore why you think so. If your reasons are sound, go for it.

The trick with recruitment is to balance risk. Your goal is to adopt a system that will give you a strong recruitment pipeline and consistently lead to excellent hires that will take your business toward your vision, while at the same time ensure that courageous decisions are taken—and taken fast. The best recruitment systems manage, quantify, and mitigate risk; they do not eliminate it. To seek to eliminate all risk in the recruitment process will box you in too tightly. While you might never make a bad hire, you might

> I can count my serious hiring mistakes over a 20-year corporate career on one hand. Each time I did not have a very good feeling but nothing sufficiently tangible to hang onto, so I went with the management consensus. This turned out to be the wrong thing every time. I should have listened to myself and pushed hard to evaluate the proposed hiring decision. Further discussion might have highlighted the flaw or poor fit and stopped the hire.

increasingly find you are not making excellent hires (or indeed any hires). The qualities that make someone a star can be elusive. They are often unconscious to the candidate and can be accompanied by some downsides. Your job is to spot the upside and the downsides and then decide if the downsides can be managed in the context of the organisational culture and structure in place today. You also need to determine if it is right for both you and the individual.

The definition of the best candidate is not fixed. It is contextual. To make great hires requires a strong understanding of this broader picture. Every top-talent professional comes with some challenges, and each of your managers should be able to cope differently with different challenges. It would be foolish to pair someone who has great potential but needs strong management with a relaxed and flexible manager. Neither will flourish, and you will have wasted a great deal of company time and money.

The final word on courage is to stick with it. Most managers are under severe pressure when they are hiring. Workload will be significantly increased not just because of the vacancy but also because of all the work involved in recruiting the replacement. Compromising on the candidate, however, is swapping a short period of intense pain (covering for the vacancy) for a long period of chronic pain (dealing with poor or mediocre performance), coupled with very significant costs (cost of hire, opportunity cost, and cost of fire). My company works with a lot of senior executives, some more capable than others, and it is clear that the ones who show courage when recruiting are the ones who are successful and will continue to be so in the future.

Do Something Today

✓ Think back over your recent hires. Is there anyone you were very tempted to hire but did not? How about someone you were persuaded to hire despite some reluctance? Track these two people down—try LinkedIn or use your HR team—and look at how their career has progressed. What can you learn from this for the future?

Remember Your 4Ps

Recruitment very closely mirrors marketing and sales. Applying the 4Ps marketing mix model provides some useful insights and opportunities. The concept is straightforward: All the elements

Treat recruitment as you would any marketing campaign. Think about E. Jerome McCarthy's 4Ps of the marketing mix:

- Product
- Place
- Price
- Promotion

Apply this to your recruitment. It is a useful way of looking at recruitment a bit differently.

are important but you can give varying weight to each one. When applied to recruitment, this works on two levels. First is the overall organisation level. If, as an organisation, you do not wish (or cannot afford) to pay salaries in the top 10%, you need to balance this out by offering more in the other quadrants. Equally, at the individual level, the 4Ps encourages you to mix the offer differently for different people. This is potentially one of the most powerful tools you can employ, and one that, properly employed, will keep you from wasting time and money on employment features that are not valued. This is broader than flexible benefits, and if properly designed can work in large companies as well as small ones.

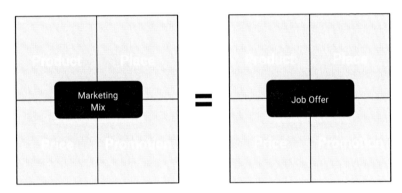

Product

What are you offering that will distinguish you from the competitors and attract talent to your job and your company?

This can be the opportunity to work with a top-branded company or the chance to join a start-up. It can be full-time, long-term employment and career prospects, or flexibility, freedom, and challenge. What about training and development? Opportunity to travel?

Some of these features will be more readily available to you than others. Consider the relative value of each from the point of view of the candidates you are trying to attract, and balance this out across the overall offer—both within the product quadrant itself and across all four quadrants.

Price

How does your pay and overall compensation/reward package compare? Are you offering better pay and benefits, wealth creation (low pay now but a share in future success of the company), or neither?

Generally, base pay is the easiest element for prospective candidates to compare, and quite often it is the only element they take into account. It is worth noting that potential candidates may not initially have a very high level of trust and confidence in the organisation, particularly when a potential employer is new and unknown to them. This leads them to be quite short-term in their outlook when deciding whether or not to take a job—or even to apply or go to an interview. If you know that your base pay is not higher than that of your competitors (and remember a competitor is not always an employer in the same sector, but someone who is looking for the same people as you), you need to raise the issue yourself so that the candidates can make a more favourable comparison using the different criteria. Be honest and say that you don't seek to compete on base pay. Ask them what is important to them. Treat them as your equals, as people the firm already wants to take seriously. Make this an Adult-to-Adult conversation. This will allow you to bring the other elements into the mix and talk about how you approach the whole employment experience rather than just one element. If someone has choices and is short-term price shopping, they will not take your job, but many other high-performing people will. As with most situations, an early *no* saves you time, money, and heartache.

The less you wish or can afford to pay, the more you need to "spend" on the other elements.

To illustrate the relationship between product and price, let's assume you are a reasonably sized (say 5,000 employees), fairly traditional company. You are based in one country only. You want to hire a top quality, ambitious, and entrepreneurial talent. You are facing some financial pressure and are worried about disrupting the internal equity of all your salaries so you want to keep base pay to the median. Your benefit package is good, and your bonus structure is pretty undifferentiating (i.e., paid out within a narrow spread). What can you do to make your "product" offer attractive to balance out your less attractive salary package?

The options are broad. To some extent, they depend on who you are trying to attract. But be conscious that your brand is broader than this one recruitment campaign. You do not want to be too radical for this one job, although in this particular example you are looking to bring someone in who is top quality, entrepreneurial, and ambitious. The first place to look is the bonus—what can you do there? Offering a high-risk compensation package separates the confident risk taker from the cautious, less confident candidate; is this approach an option, or are you still worried about internal equity? How about putting together a fast-track development programme that includes the individual getting quality commercial training and education over the first three years? Will this work for you?

Advertise the job internally with this training offer displayed transparently, and you have sorted out your internal equity concerns. Think longer term, however, and remember that you might want to do something to ensure the person doesn't walk at the end of the three years. For example, is a big promotion realistic if you recruit the right person? If so, plan it in and make sure you are in a position to deliver. The thinking goes on from there.

You should also balance this out with the other quadrants. Think about how much weight this quadrant realistically carries, and this will tell you how much extra value you need to put into it or can take from the other quadrants.

Place

What can you do here that gives you an edge? Can you be flexible in terms of times of work, location of work, working from home? Is your business located in a low- or high-cost area? Is there high or low unemployment? What are the available skills? Is there a local university or college that you can build a strong relationship with to maintain a strong candidate pipeline?

To illustrate this, let's use the example that you are in a high-cost area and you have found that keeping top talent has proved challenging. Is there anything you can do to stimulate getting your recruits into the local housing market? This will make your offer attractive and also lock people in for the long term. Clearly this is a costly option so it needs to be carefully managed, but it can give you a real edge in a competitive marketplace. Think also about hiring people at the start of their careers when they are more flexible on location and do not have to accommodate a family, then develop them for more senior jobs within the organisation. Consider options for remote working or working from home if people have a long commute. This does not work for everyone. Once again, these factors need to be well-managed (people earn the right by demonstrating they can make it work), but if you can, come up with a unique offer that will give you an edge over your local competitors.

Promotion

How do you plan to attract people? There is a simple balance here: cash vs. time. The more time you can put into it, the lower the cost. Remember that your competitors for top talent are not always in the same industry. Think creatively about where you could find the people you need. Recruiting for attitude and aptitude means that you can, for some roles, be wide-thinking about candidate sources. The more flexible and creative you are, the bigger the talent pool from which to select.

Differentiate yourself by the way that you recruit. Do the opposite of your competitors for top talent. For example, if you are up against majors who are known to take a long time hiring, be super fast.

This example of great, flexible, candidate-centric recruitment is personal to me. Many years ago I was applying for a role in a new part of the country (having decided to follow my husband and give up my current role to do so). As can happen with someone actively looking for a new job, I ended up with two interviews for two very different roles at the same time. I went to an interview on Monday with one role and then Tuesday for the other. Tuesday afternoon, the Monday interview contacted me and offered me the role. I contacted the Tuesday interviewing manager and explained that I had received another offer and wanted to check where they were in the process so I could decide what to do. Her response was that they had two candidates and had been planning to invite me back to a second interview the following week. However, given that I had another offer, she suggested that I come down for the second interview that evening. To help me with my decision, they would decide about me immediately rather than ask me to wait for their interview with the other candidate.

I set off straight away to the interview, which involved two business managers plus the person with whom I had previously interviewed. At the end of the interview, before even leaving the room, I was offered the role. This is an example of being candidate-centric (see Chapter 3). Both roles were similar in terms of package and challenge, although quite different in job content. The choice would normally have been quite hard, but this is the one that struck a chord. This was the type of organisation I wanted to join.

> ## Do Something Today
>
> ✓ Have a look at your company 4Ps for recruitment.
> Are you missing an opportunity or two? Has your
> organisation sunk into a "this is how we do things
> around here" rut? What can be shaken up?

Hiring Hourglass

The marketing hourglass can be applied to the hiring process and offers a useful model to put your hiring activities into context.

KNOW	**Know:** The first stage of hiring is ensuring you are known to your target hires. They need to know who you are and what you stand for.
LIKE	**Like:** Next, they need to agree with your purpose and values and want to be associated with your brand.
TRUST	**Trust:** They need to trust you as a recruiter and as an employer.
TRY	**Try:** This is the experiential part of your hiring process, when they meet you and their potential manager and colleagues.
BUY	**Buy:** This is when they accept your offer.
REMAIN	**Remain:** Here they agree that the decision to join was the right one and that they want to remain and contribute.
REFER	**Refer:** Here they want to bring their friends in to work with you.

Do Something Today

✓ Score yourself on a 1–10 scale against each of these
processes. Be critical and think of it from the point
of view of a winner whom you want to hire. Where
are you doing well and where do you need to focus
some attention?

Be Systematic

*Systematising your hiring process will not only
save time and effort but also lead to improving
your process and thus your chances of consistently
hiring A-Players ahead of your competition.*

Hiring talent is a process, and you therefore need to develop and
follow a system. The benefits of having a system include:

- Consistency
- Replicability
- Trainability
- Measurability
- Improvability

Consistency helps the people involved in hiring—managers,
HR, administration—since they will know what they need to do
and when. The process then requires less mental effort and less

energy and creates better results. Consistency requires a clear process and clear templates. It creates habits of good behaviour.

Replicability means that you can continuously achieve the same results. You can involve more or new staff in the process and still achieve the same results. You are therefore less dependent on individuals without whom your process would collapse.

Trainability of how you recruit impacts quality and consistency but also the candidate experience. It is critical that you offer a challenging but high-quality experience to all candidates. If you want to hire them, this will play a key part in their decision to take the role. If you do not wish to hire them, their experience will be widely shared among the community from which you will likely be hiring. Not getting an offer from a company where the recruitment experience was high quality is quite different from not getting an offer when the experience was poor.

Measurability is key to improvement. If you do not know what the process is, you cannot measure it. Therefore, being systematic allows you to measure results.

Improvability is then possible. Following a system allows you to measure and improve and therefore achieve higher performance and better results.

When developing your recruitment process, it is useful to clearly indicate who has responsibility for which element. This reduces overlap or gaps. Below is a short example.

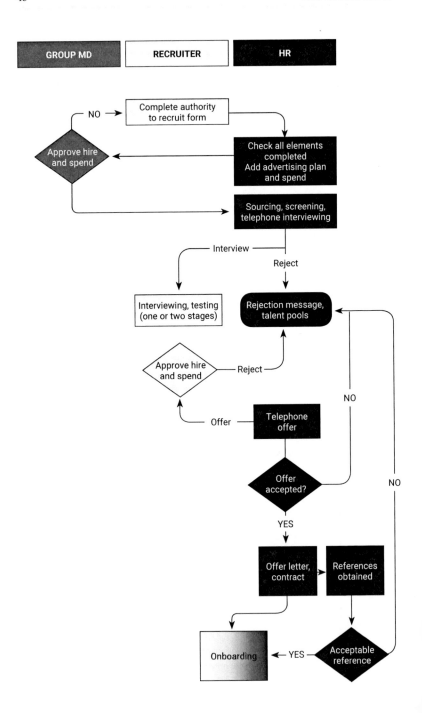

Do Something Today

✓ Try jotting down your current recruitment process and identifying those areas in which you think you are most/least effective. Test this with some recent recruits.

Recruitment Timescales

It is good practice to have an agreed set of deadlines that can be used to create specific timescales within each hiring campaign. It enables a better plan and sets expectations.

The following illustrates a typical example of timescales an HR or in-house recruitment team might want to agree on with the recruiting manager. It is key that time is planned for shortlisting, interviewing, etc., at the beginning of the process. Otherwise delays will occur at every stage, and, as we will explore in more detail later, delays can lead to you losing the best candidates.

Once the deadlines and timescales have been agreed upon, they need to be added to the programme and tracked. Part of the post-recruitment review will be to evaluate if the deadlines were met by all parties involved.

Task	Who does what (Responsible person)	Timetable
Complete authorisation process	Get recruiting manager's signature	Same day or if not available maximum two days.
Internal advertisement	HR	Same day vacancy approved.
External advertisement	HR to create and recruiting manager to approve	Five days to produce and sign off.
Closing date for applications to be decided and added to advertisement	HR to manage advertising and applications	Not less than two weeks.
Time between closing date and selection for interview	Manager to pre-book dates	Recommend not more than three days.
Time between selection and initial phone interview	Manager to pre-book dates	Recommend not more than three days.
Candidate to complete online psychometric tests; timing to be agreed as either before phone interview or before face-to-face interview	Recruiting manager and HR to agree on timing; HR to administer	Candidates given two days to complete.
Time between initial phone interview and face-to-face interviews	Manager to pre-book dates	Recommend not more than three days.
Time between interview and decision	Manager to decide	Recommend not more than three days.
Time between decision advised to HR, papers returned, details of terms and conditions confirmed, and production of offer letter	HR to produce	External: Three days. Internal: One day. Ready in afternoon if told in the morning. Ready in the morning if told in the afternoon.
Production of turndown letters (after advised of decision and papers returned)	HR to produce	External: Five days. Internal: One day.
Contract available (external)	HR to produce	With offer letter (exceptionally on first day of work).
Evaluation of exercise	HR to undertake	Two weeks from date of completion of campaign.

Recruitment Programme

Before starting any recruitment campaign, you need to set up the programme. Not only will this keep you on track but it will also hold the participants accountable.

The programme should be set up in discussion with the key people involved: HR and the recruiting manager. It is important to put in completion dates at the outset of the campaign and then to add the actual achieved dates as you go through the process. This is not to create opportunities for blame but to ensure that the time needed is properly scheduled. If you know when you expect to shortlist or interview you can book time for this in your schedule and not let the process slip. At the end of the process it provides information for your process review. Learning is essential if your recruitment activities are to be as efficient and effective as possible.

It also ensures that you do not have long gaps in the process. There is very little that annoys a candidate more than extensive delays and waiting. Top talent will not tolerate this and will simply take a role with a different employer.

Manager name		HR name	
Vacancy reference		Job title of vacancy	
Authorisation submitted (date)		Authorisation received (date)	
Internal or external ad	Internal yes/no External yes/no	If external, where?	
Advertisement date		Closing date?	
Preferred start date			
Job description	Yes/no	Person specifications	Yes/no
Interview panel		Psychometrics	
Planned interview dates			
Terms and conditions agreed	Yes/no	Relocation support	Yes/no
Qualifications required		Proof obtained	

	Planned	Actual
Date CVs sent to recruiting manager		
Date shortlisted candidates sent to HR		
Date reject letters sent out, if applicable		
Date for psychometrics		
Date for interviews		
Date of selection decision meeting		
Date offer letter issued		

Recruitment and the Success Triangle

The Success Triangle was designed to support salespeople, but it also applies to the world of recruitment. The idea here is that success is the result of the convergence of three core elements:

- **Attitude:** outlook and expectations; confidence and conviction.
- **Technique:** strategies and tactics; knowing the right thing to do and say in a given situation.
- **Behaviour:** actually doing the right things on a consistent basis; "muscle memory."

This section will explore the behaviour, attitude, and techniques/skills you will be looking for in your candidates. First is behaviour, since that's the most immediately noticeable of the three and an easy entry point, with a focus primarily on sales, since the bottom-line impact in this realm of hiring is particularly easy to demonstrate. The same basic principles, however, apply to all positions for which you are hiring.

Behaviour

Behaviour means the actions and processes routinely used by the individual in carrying out their role. Winning behaviour is that which enables the individual to perform their role effectively.

The quick establishment of bonding and rapport with others, for instance, is an essential behaviour of Winners in all fields. It is particularly important in the world of sales. So you should notice: Does the sales candidate warm to others quickly? They should be assertive, but not aggressive. Bonding should not be put ahead of selling. Successful salespeople, for instance, understand and are able to cope with the fact that selling is not about getting one's own emotional needs met. It is about discovering the prospect's emotional needs and being trustworthy enough for them to be comfortable opening up to you. An A-Player knows how and when to bond and builds rapport throughout the sales meeting. Non-Winners feel they must bond socially, which tends to make them somewhat subservient. An A-Player is never emotionally involved in making the sale.

Handling emotions effectively is another key behaviour to consider when hiring salespeople. When you are emotionally involved in a sale, you are out of control. A-Players remain objective, and they listen. Ideal candidates know how to keep their emotions in check without appearing cold and distant. Warmth (not coldness) and assertiveness (not aggressiveness or submissiveness) are the ideal combination.

Strong candidates in all positions will be able to give evidence of highly focused, goal-oriented behaviours; this is an essential behaviour for salespeople. Ask for examples of times when they worked systematically toward a goal that they achieved despite things not always going the way they hoped. Their focus and systematic approach means that they are able to keep the sales process on track no matter what the prospect throws at them.

One of the challenges with "natural" or maverick salespeople is that while they might be successful, they are not generally that systematic. This means that they don't really know what works and what does not work. They are unlikely to have faced adversity either, which can make them incapable of maintaining motivation and performance if they are not winning. Maverick salespeople tend to be untrainable—they don't feel the need to learn. When recruiting, you are looking for people with the attitude and behaviours that will lead to strong and consistent performance.

It is also critical when recruiting to establish whether your candidate has the ethics of a Winner. This requires clear examples of acting honestly and professionally when it would have been easy to act otherwise. This can be hard to determine in an interview—after all, few candidates if asked the direct question will say they have poor ethics—but exploring past behaviour can give you insights. Look for examples of when candidates pulled back from something that was not in the best interest of the other party, despite a cost to themselves.

Some examples of desirable behaviours:

- Is goal-oriented.
- Plans activities.
- Takes action.
- Manages time and resources effectively.
- Is structured and well-organised.

Attitude

A-Players in the world of sales (and elsewhere) are unconditionally committed to doing what it takes to succeed with commitment, passion, desire, and self-belief. They understand that success means working at the edge of their comfort zones, and they see discomfort as a signal that growth is happening.

Winners are persistent in the face of difficulties. They know they will succeed even if they aren't exactly sure how. Determination and drive indicate the candidates' will to win.

Winners know that selling is about going to the bank. They are comfortable with the fact that they will be well-compensated for a job well done. Salespeople who are motivated by being liked, being heard, making friends, or being seen as an expert will struggle when the time comes to hold their ground and keep the prospect in the process. Salespeople who are uncomfortable with the concept of money will struggle to make any, both in terms of holding their nerve on price (i.e., not discounting) but also in terms of achieving consistent personal sales performance. This is not about crass self-enrichment at the expense of the prospect, but a legitimate desire to make money and to enjoy the benefits of doing so (whether this is for charitable works, fast cars, or security for the family).

Winners are energised by interaction with others but they are not seeking approval or acceptance from them. They are seeking solutions that are good for both the prospect and themselves. For them, winning means having fun while helping prospects with what they are seeking to accomplish.

It takes courage to do what it takes to be a Winner. Combined with emotional intelligence, courage produces assertiveness that attracts people and does not put them off.

Some examples of desirable attitudes:

- High self-esteem (but not arrogant).
- Motivation.
- Drive for success.
- Self-discipline.
- Enthusiasm, passion.
- Openness to change.
- Openness to constructive feedback; strong self-development orientation.
- Taking responsibility.

Technique

A-Players in the world of sales know the value of regular, effective prospecting. They make calls and engage in prospecting activities on a regular basis. They also understand the value of referrals and contacts as a source of prospects. They prospect consistently rather than in spurts when the pipeline is empty. Winners understand that a full pipeline gives them choice, and they put in the effort to achieve this.

Winners know how to handle stalls, objections, and put-offs. Not only do they spot them, but they also address them. They ask simple, testing questions without upsetting the prospect. They subscribe to the rule: "If you feel it, say it, gently." Non-Winners allow their need for approval to get in the way. Winners help prospects say "no," confront a prospect who is leading them on, and ask the necessary questions to progress the sale. To facilitate the prospects' decision making, Winners are not focused on the actual decision (the *yes* or the *no*) but on the process of making a decision. The salespeople you will be looking for will know that only prospects can overcome their own objections; they don't defend and justify or try to encourage a sale through pitching features and benefits. They stick with the process.

A winning salesperson understands the importance of listening in the sales communication process. Using active listening for this kind of salesperson is automatic. Look for evidence in the interview stage of strong, active listening skills. Behavioural interviewing is perfect for this (questions such as: "What did they say, and then what did you do?").

Some examples of desirable techniques displayed:

- Builds rapport easily with others.
- Is a good communicator, good listener.
- Takes a systematic approach to selling.
- Uses multiple channels for prospecting.
- Keeps the sale on track and the sales cycle as short as possible.
- Facilitates the prospects' overcoming their stalls and objections.

The Success Triangle for Recruiters

When recruiting for your team or organisation, you should also embody the ideal behaviours, attitudes, and techniques required for success within the role you have taken on.

Recruitment Behaviour

Behaviour in the recruitment context relates to having a systematic approach to the task at hand or a step-by-step plan for reaching the goals through disciplined action that has been planned. In terms of recruitment, behaviour is all about having a planned, structured approach and sticking to it. It means keeping the employee value proposition in the forefront of everything that you do and taking full advantage of opportunities to increase the talent within your organisation.

Recruitment Attitude

Attitude has to do with your outlook—the perception you have about yourself, your company, your product or service, and your marketplace. Your attitude can be one of possibility or one of limitation. Since it's your perception, it's your choice. In terms of recruitment, attitude communicates itself to potential candidates in a myriad of ways. People want to join teams in which people have a positive attitude toward themselves, each other, the company, and its products or services. Recruiting managers with a strong positive attitude find it easier to bring in top talent.

Recruitment Technique

Technique relates to skills. It consists of the strategies, tactics, and personal presence (strength) you use to implement your behaviour plan. In terms of recruitment, technique means having the skills to screen CVs, conduct effective interviews, and spot talent—and also spot people who talk a good story but will not deliver. Technique is developed through training, practice, and self-reflection/learning.

Hiring Salespeople

The Success Triangle can also be applied to your definition of the ideal candidate, your A-Player or Winner. Regardless of the specific sales role, all great salespeople have this in common: They have an extraordinary desire to excel, to do more, and to continually improve. In short, they have a winning attitude. This desire to win in turn drives the actions—the behaviours—required to win.

Having the right attitude, practicing the right behaviour, and learning and practicing proven sales techniques leads to success—consistent, strong sales performance. With the right technique,

salespeople can increase their winning ratio significantly over less
proficient colleagues.

Four key attributes of winning salespeople are:

- Will to win.
- Strong internal motivation.
- Strong self-discipline.
- Ability to nurture and grow relationships.

Your success in building a winning sales team depends on your
ability to recruit A-Players (or Winners) with these four attributes.

Will to Win

Salespeople with a will to win understand that if they want to
sell more, they have to fail more. They keep going regardless of
the number of *noes* they receive. They don't get discouraged. They
understand that you don't win in sales by getting only *yesses*; you
win in sales by getting *noes*. If your prospect gives you a *no*, you've
eliminated a non-productive lead before it has wasted your time.

Of course, getting a *yes* is ideal. But it's essential to discover
noes early in the game. Winning salespeople aren't afraid to fail;
their self-concept can handle it. They recognise that a *no* represents a step toward the *yes*. They believe in their product, they
believe they offer benefit and value to the buyer, and they have an
attitude of abundance and confidence that there are more than
enough people out there who want to buy their product or service
and will benefit from it. They are focused on doing whatever it
takes—consistent with strong ethical principles—to get the sale.

When interviewing, your job is to find out about the candidate's
attitude to failure and adversity. Do they persevere or do they give
up? Have they experienced failure and built resilience or has it all
come easily to them? In a strange way when hiring salespeople, a

bit of failure may not be a bad thing when coupled with a strong will to win, strong internal motivation, strong self-discipline, and the ability to build rapport (as an equal not a friend).

Strong Internal Motivation

People work for different reasons: money, recognition, building relationships, breaking their own records, excelling over others, etc. Your ideal candidates will have their own internal motivation or combination of motives. The trick in recruiting is to uncover this motivation and to determine if it is something that you can cultivate with the right support and stimulation. You cannot motivate anyone to do anything but you can create the right environment (support, challenge, incentives) for people to motivate themselves, provided they have strong internal motivation. Thus, part of your recruitment effort must be to establish the strength of motivation as well as the actual motivators themselves.

Strong Self-Discipline

In order to succeed in sales, a salesperson needs solid organisational skills, a good work ethic, and the discipline to keep it going. Remember that "discipline equals freedom." When recruiting salespeople, you need to find people who want the freedom that comes from discipline. Being prepared to set up a 90-day plan and then work that plan is a core ingredient to superior selling. Finding evidence that the candidate will be amenable to this is important during the recruitment process.

Ability to Nurture and Grow Relationships

High-performing salespeople have the emotional intelligence and interpersonal skills to quickly build rapport with prospects. Much of this derives from having the confidence to be relaxed and deeply listen to the prospect, seeking to truly hear and understand them. People want to know that you understand their problems from their point of view, not just from yours.

This must not be confused with trying to be their friend. In sales, it is about establishing a strong relationship based on mutual respect, one of parity or equal business stature. When recruiting, you need to be looking for people with the gravitas to be their own person while in the service of the prospect or client.

Do Something Today

✓ Create your list of the behaviours, attitudes, and techniques of your ideal salesperson and then review your salespeople against this.

Chapter Summary

This chapter has explored the strategy and context required for excellence in recruitment. Key messages include:

- Recruitment is both an art and a science. You need to understand and master both aspects.
- Understanding the cost of error in recruitment, both direct and indirect, is essential. It provides the motivation to hold your nerve and not compromise when making a hiring decision.
- Taking a strategic and longer term view will enable you to build organisational capability and prepare your organisation for long-term growth and success.

- Recruitment needs to be defined in the much broader framework of talent management, ensuring that you can fill positions with the right candidates in a timely and effective manner.
- Be courageous—hire people that are different from you, with higher potential. Keep on searching until you find the right candidate, and don't compromise.
- Think about your 4Ps of recruitment: your offer (product); your compensation/reward package (price); your working arrangements and location (place); and your approach to attracting candidates (promotion).
- Think about your hiring hourglass: know, like, trust, try, buy, remain, refer.
- Be systematic. This will save you time and improve your process, increasing your changing of consistently hiring A-Players ahead of your competition.
- Establish up front of a recruitment campaign the programme, timetable, and deadlines; review this at the end.
- Remember the three points of the Success Triangle: behaviour, attitude, and technique. Apply this to your approach to recruitment. You can also use it when defining your candidates.

CHAPTER 3

Culture and Attitude

rganisational culture and attitude is a constant theme
across the employee lifecycle from recruiting to retir-
ing. It is not something that you can fix or change overnight; equally, it is something that will happen with or without
your intervention. It is experiential—you cannot write down the
culture you want and then have it. You need to communicate
intent (aspirations) and then take action that is congruent with
that intent.

Some of your culture is underground. You need to foster
a climate of trust to be able to hear about it, let alone affect it.
Taking culture seriously and improving it over time is a long-
term commitment that will bring significant rewards in terms of
recruitment and in other pursuits as well.

Recruiting Culture

The most effective approach for gaining new talent is to build a corporate-wide culture of recruiting in which every manager and employee is a recruiter.

Because of their continuous contact and interaction with outside talent, team members play an important supplemental role in identifying talent and spreading the employment brand. The most effective recruiting strategies convince employees to be talent scouts, making every employee a recruiter. (See also Chapter 5, the "Finding: Efficient, Effective, and Creative Sourcing" section.)

Part of building a strong recruiting culture is to invest in training your managers in recruitment. Best practices include ensuring that your recruitment training is a pass/fail programme. Include evaluation in the programme; managers must be formally accredited as competent before they start to recruit. Unaccredited managers can co-interview with accredited managers or HR staff but should not be left to do this alone.

It is unusual to have pass/fail in any sort of management training or development programme, but when it comes to recruitment this will set a high standard and send a strong message. Recruitment is both an art and a science. People need to be able to demonstrate competence before they are allowed to impact candidates and the long-term success of the business.

Candidate-Centric

As mentioned previously, recruitment has many similarities to selling. Indeed, at any one point during a recruitment campaign, there is always a seller and a buyer. The role, however, is not fixed, and many recruiters fall at the first hurdle. Namely, they consider themselves the buyer and that they have something of greater value in the transaction, namely a job. However, when seeking top talent, you will find that the candidate has something of at least equal if not greater value, namely their talent.

Recruiters will fare better if they spend more of their time thinking of themselves in the seller role—the non-traditional seller, naturally. Don't fall into the trap of pitching the "features and benefits" of your company and the role you are looking to fill. Rather, properly investigate the candidates' interests and suitability for the role. Asking questions is the way to do this.

There are four key elements to being candidate-centric:

- Focus on the candidates' needs, their job selection criteria, and their hiring experience.
- Sell the candidates on applying for and accepting the job.
- Build relationships (candidate pools, alumni, etc.).
- Make fast recruiting decisions for high-demand candidates.

Focus on the Candidate

Focus on the candidate needs to start at the very beginning of the recruitment process and is integral to each aspect, from finding to attracting to interviewing to offering.

The impact of getting this wrong and creating a negative candidate experience is much more than simply losing a top-quality candidate. You run the risk of losing people within that candidate's immediate and extended network. With social networks as extensive as they are, each candidate's extended network is considerably wide. The adage that a shopper who has a bad shopping experience tells at least ten people about it applies equally to a candidate who has a bad interviewing experience. These days, of course, telling ten people includes posting the message on social media. If the candidate is sufficiently motivated, there are a number of forums and sites where the news can be spread and will be checked by other potential applicants.

There is a lot of evidence that candidates like to be stretched during an interview. They correlate this with interest and challenge. You must always protect their dignity, and the process needs to feel fair. Candidates who are rigorously interviewed by recruiters who have done their homework and thought about the questions will most likely consider it a good experience whether or not they are given a job offer. A 25-minute chat as the interviewer glances at the CV for the first time while asking softball questions is not going to rank very well.

Some suggestions:

- Think about your ideal candidates and what is going to appeal to them when you craft job advertisements. Your advert wants to attract ideal candidates and put off those who do not qualify, as indeed any marketing campaign is designed to do.

- Remember, however, that adverts will be read by all your potential candidates, not only those who are interested in that particular vacancy. You cannot change your tone of voice radically from advert to advert since this will confuse and most likely put people off. The need to have a clear value proposition is critical if consistent messages are to be communicated to all potential employees.

- The process from the point of application to communicating the decision needs to be thought through, planned, and templated. Time passes quickly for recruiters who are handling lots of applications and doing lots of other things, including, for line managers, their day job. For candidates, especially those who are taking the application seriously (rather than pressing the apply-all button on a job site), each day that passes feels like a long time. Therefore, when planning the process, you need to consider the touch points and the gaps and manage these effectively.

- Templating—acknowledgment emails, invitations to interview, turn downs, etc.—enables not just greater efficiency but also the ability to think about the message and impact in advance when you have time. It also improves consistency and reduces the risk of missing something or wording something badly in haste. Candidates are more likely to scrutinise messages than the sender and thus pick up on typos and errors (and not be impressed).

- Streamline and continually review your recruitment processes. A lengthy, time-consuming, or unsatisfactory process often puts top talent off from either applying (if the process is too onerous), attending the interview (if it requires too much time off their current work), or accepting the job (if they did not feel stretched and stimulated).

Selling the Candidate

Selling does not have to equate to being "salesy." Indeed there is nothing a candidate likes less than an overzealous, over-salesy approach during a recruitment process or interview. If you are salesy, you run the risk of sounding inauthentic or desperate. Neither commends itself to the candidate. Inauthenticity puts people's backs up and makes them suspicious—nothing can be as good as it sounds. Desperation is even worse. Not only do people not like to surround themselves with desperate people, but it also raises suspicions.

So why am I talking about selling to the candidate? Two reasons.

First, this is about mindset. If you go into recruitment thinking that "they [the candidates] are lucky to be given a chance," you will have the wrong tonality. You will consciously or unconsciously give out the message that you are the superior and the candidate is the inferior. People don't like to feel this way. Only the desperate would be willing to take a job when that's the positioning from the outset. Second, the truth is that top talent has choices. Your job therefore is to make it easy for top candidates to choose you.

When I talk about selling, I talk about the process in which you use the questions you ask to demonstrate that you are the company to join. Use your knowledge of candidates to ask questions that both enable you to find out if they are suitable for you but also make them want to be part of the team. The recruitment process and specifically the recruitment interview includes encouraging candidates' desire to be part of your team. You do this by being prepared, professional, and authentic.

Essentially, for a candidate to accept your job offer, they have to make a change. The best explanation of what is required for change is the Change Equation popularised by David Gleicher. This equation states that change is a function of three variables. The sum of these variables needs to be greater than or at least equal to the resistance to that change. One key aspect is that variables are multiplied, which means that if any variable is missing the momentum for change becomes zero (because anything multiplied by zero is zero).

Some candidates may arrive fully mobilised and ready to make a move. This does not, however, mean that they are not making a change. Therefore, the equation still applies. Their dissatisfaction with the present may be fully established (they want to move away from their old position, whether as an employee, a student, or unemployed). For those who currently have a job, they may

$$\text{Change} = f \frac{\substack{\text{Dissatisfaction} \\ \text{with the present}} \times \substack{\text{Vision of} \\ \text{the future}} \times \substack{\text{First} \\ \text{practical} \\ \text{steps}}}{\geq \substack{\text{Cost} \\ \text{Pain} \\ \text{Effort}} \text{[Resistance]}}$$

want new challenges. It could be a move dictated by the need to relocate. The impetus for change, regardless of how it manifests itself, is still dissatisfaction with the present situation. Other candidates may not be quite so sure. They may simply be curious at the start.

Your job, therefore, is to establish if there is current dissatisfaction and to understand its nature. Making assumptions at this stage can be dangerous and lead to a failed hiring process. Remember that candidates will not necessarily feel able to be open to sharing their dissatisfactions (although, bizarrely, some can be somewhat too willing) so you need to be patient and gentle to get to the truth. Using negative reverses can be quite powerful. "It sounds like you have a great job and would really struggle to leave it. Tell me more about that."

Facilitating an understanding of the candidates' vision of their future is an important part of effective interviewing. Not only does it help candidates conclude that you are the right next move for them, but it also enables you to match their vision to yours and to see if there is sufficient correlation to make this a good hire. Additionally, the gap between their vision of their future and their current position can create or amplify dissatisfaction with the present.

Compensation will come into this future vision, but although it is important information to gather, it is rarely the most important consideration.

One of the best ways to describe a job is to talk about the key expectations for the first 12 months. This will make the job tangible, shift the focus to outputs and achievements and away from a potentially boring list of tasks, and clearly set your expectations.

Whenever possible, give new hires responsibility. For example, during their first month, they could be asked to develop a sales plan and forecast for the first year. This will be supported by their manager. They will have access to existing plans, but you want them to take responsibility for their performance from the get-go.

The first practical steps are fairly straightforward in recruitment and need little more than talking through the process with the candidates. However, don't end the process you are describing at the point of the offer. Your ability to demonstrate a strong onboarding plan will go a long way to selling your opportunity. Too often companies omit a discussion of onboarding, which is not only damaging to them but also removes a valuable element from the job offer. Talking about training, career development, and future challenges can also make you an attractive future employer.

Be honest. There is no point in tricking someone into joining your company. Candidates will not take long to find out what the real truth is, and, apart from the damage to trust, you could find yourself with problem employees who do not want the job in which you placed them.

Resistance to change in a recruitment situation is fairly straightforward to identify—the discomfort of leaving something you know, people you like, bosses you have loyalty to, coupled with the risk of starting somewhere new, and in some companies and countries losing the security or rewards that come through service. These factors need to be explored during the recruitment process. If they are not, the risk of making an offer and then not understanding why it has not been accepted increases.

Build Relationships

Building relationships, which we will look at more in the next chapter, is about maximising the recruitment process. Being candidate-centric includes thinking about the longer term. Just because valued employees may leave you, it does not mean that they should be no longer valued (or indeed valuable). Top employees can leave for good reasons, and if treated well they can become a recruit in the future. They can also become a talent scout or ambassador, sending people your way. Individuals who have a good recruitment experience regardless of getting an offer will tell their friends and contacts to consider you for their next move. Chances are they will have some talented people in their circle.

Move from transactional to relational recruitment. Transactional recruitment is highly efficient but low touch. It focuses on the recruitment activity itself and short-term recruitment to find the best candidate for the role being filled. Relational recruitment takes the long-term view and sees recruitment interactions in the broader context, including brand building, talent spotting, and quality decision making based on an intimate knowledge and understanding of the candidates.

Looking at the recruitment flow—from search/attraction to pre-screening, selection, offer, and deployment—the intensity of interaction between the hiring party and the candidate builds, achieving its highest peak probably at Day 1 and during the onboarding phase. Here the candidate is not unlike a sales prospect. Rapport building continues throughout the process, building to the point of full commitment. Here the product/service "sold" is the job offer and starting employment with your company.

Speed

I am personally not a fan of the approach of dragging applicants through 20 interviews, 14 peer reviews, and a bunch of other hurdles all to make sure they are a good "fit." I believe that if you are skilled at interviewing and spotting potential, you can make a good recruitment decision a lot quicker than that. You may have a brand where people are queuing up to join, in which case you can choose to have a bit of fun making yourself exclusive. But I cannot stop myself thinking that this is evidence of poor talent spotting or inadequate performance predicting capability. Also, for some people with strong alternatives, too long a chase will put them off, no matter the brand.

As an aside, I also have strong reservations about peer interviewing. Certainly, meeting some colleagues can be central to a good recruitment experience, but allowing peers to select makes me a little nervous. It is not so much that peers won't hire competition (i.e., someone who might be better than them or go further than them) since if you have a high-performing culture this might not get in the way (or at least not consciously); it is more that peers might not be able to spot superior talent and that they might recruit "people like us." This will ultimately create a non-diverse team with all the resultant performance limitations that comes with this.

Recruitment needs to be a two-way process—candidate and employer must mutually benefit from the hiring decision. Therefore, building into your process a real opportunity to meet colleagues and get to know the job can be a very effective way to attract top talent. This can happen pre- or post-selection. Pre-selection is to arrange for them to meet colleagues as part of the formal interviewing process. This can work and will not do you any harm, but it can feel a bit artificial. Candidates and team members will be very aware of what is happening, which makes it feel a bit staged. Sometimes team members, in an effort to be collaborative and collegiate, may go a bit over the top, either positively (too enthusiastic about the company/job) or negatively (hyper-challenging and testing).

An alternative is to allow the candidate who has been offered the job a chance to meet the team prior to making a decision to accept. This will strongly reinforce the message that you see this as a two-way street and that you want the candidate to make an informed decision. It also signals clearly that you have nothing to hide and that the candidate will be allowed to look around. This needs to be done intelligently, of course. One of my recruitment consultant clients once shared with me an example of a sales director interviewing with a competitor's manager and persuading him to give a demo of the company's latest product about to be launched. The sales director later turned down the job but now had the information.

The benefits of speed are clear to me. Looking again to sales, selling is the facilitation of three transformations: moving someone from "possibly, one day, with someone" to "definitely,

now, and with you." If you warm someone up to the idea of changing jobs—so they go to "definitely" and "now"—but you are too
slow to offer, you will miss out on the "with you" part.

This is particularly important if you are head hunting either via
external recruitment agencies or your own processes. If someone
who has not been thinking about changing jobs is warmed up and
ready for a change, they will now be open if another offer comes
in while you are deciding.

A speedy decision is often linked in the mind of the candidate
with decisiveness, clarity, and also desire and belief (for them and
in them), all of which adds to your attractiveness as a recruiter.

Trust

One of my best hires as an HR director for a large multi-
national was also one of my fastest hires. We were hiring a top
researcher from a competitor. The process started with a dinner
with the potential manager and also the SVP/Research and SVP/
Development.

The candidate over dinner stopped himself a number of times
from talking further with the words "for confidentiality reasons I
cannot talk more about this." This was reasonable and no less than
what we would have wanted one of our top scientists to do were
they interviewing.

At the end of the meal, we had a brief discussion once the
candidate had been chauffeured off to his hotel. We agreed that
there was little information to be gathered through interviews; he
was either as good as his reputation or not, and it was not going
to be possible to get the data to prove this either way. Therefore,
the next morning at 8 A.M. when he came in for his interview, we
simply made him an offer.

Clearly these were special circumstances, but our ability to turn around an offer overnight meant that the next morning I sat down and talked terms with him and he signed up. Our speed and approach did a lot to close the deal.

The good news: He turned out to be an exceptional hire, opening up some new avenues of research that did not overlap with the work he had done previously (which was tied up in non-competes).

Trust is an important component in successful hiring. Maister, Green, and Galford developed the Trust Equation in their book *The Trusted Advisor*. The equation was developed to help select advisors but can be equally applied to a number of situations, including sales, leadership, and hiring.

$$\frac{\text{Credibility} + \text{Reliability} + \text{Intimacy}}{\text{Self-Interest}} = \textbf{Trust}$$

In hiring, the elements can be defined as follows:

- **Credibility.** Your credibility when hiring derives from a number of factors: the firm itself, its brand and reputation, its website, and its social presence. The interviewers contribute also in terms of how prepared they are, how knowledgeable, and how competent; the quality of questions they ask and insights they offer; and their overall interviewing competence. Their perceived credibility, in line with communication in general, is affected not just by what they say but also how they sound and look—words, yes, but also body language and tonality.

- **Reliability.** The quality of your recruitment process impacts most heavily on the reliability score. Are your communications timely? Do you keep your promises? If you commit to responding or giving a decision within two days, you need to keep to this to avoid doing damage to your reliability score. Reliability is all about action—what you do. Do you start the interview when you say you will? Do you respond within the committed to or reasonable timeframe?

- **Intimacy.** The contributing elements to intimacy when hiring include: how well you get to know the candidate, how well you seem to know your clients, and how well you seem to know your staff. The first is about the quality and depth of questions you ask; the latter two about the information you give to a candidate. It is also about how well you seem to understand the needs and interests of the candidate. Skilled interviewers can create intimacy fast and maintain this throughout the process. Intimacy requires honesty and is rewarded with honesty.

- **Self-Interest.** This is about being perceived to be acting in your own self-interest. It's reasonable to have some self-interest; it just can't be exclusive. At the outset of a hiring process, a candidate will typically perceive the recruiter as having high self-interest. You can reinforce or increase this starting perception or you can reduce it. Increasing it is easy; simply talk a lot about yourself, the wonderfulness of the company, its many accolades, happy staff, brilliant jobs, and fantastic bonuses. Reducing it is a bit trickier but requires clear communication, an authentic style, congruence across the process, and a demonstrated understanding that this is a two-way process and that the candidate has rights and needs and must have the information required to make the right decision about acceptance.

Thus, when recruiting, you need to take into account the elements of the Trust Equation and ensure that you are not inadvertently eroding credibility, reliability, or intimacy, or communicating too much self-interest.

Always Be Recruiting

Companies that limit themselves to recruiting only when they have a specific vacancy limit their access to top talent.

Even small companies, which cannot sensibly carry additional staff without this visibly impacting the bottom line, can still be actively talent scouting and planning to recruit top talent for the future. The key to success here is keeping in touch so that when the time is right for both parties the offer can be closed. (See Chapter 5, "Pipeline Management.")

For larger companies, my advice is that if you come across unmissable candidates, you should think about how you can restructure to accommodate them. Get them in, interview them, discover their ambitions, and then get to work finding them a challenging opportunity.

Remember also that some top-talent candidates you meet might not be looking for a role just at that moment. You want to build a relationship so that when they are looking, they give you a call.

People who run sales teams know that they will always have people leaving. Therefore, there is no time when they should not be looking for the next salesperson to bring in. Work on this continuously and have some candidates in the wings so that losing a salesperson will not have such a negative impact on sales.

Additionally, as will be covered in the next chapter, you should be forecasting future demand and recruiting to this in advance.

Employee Value Proposition

In sales, a value proposition provides the concrete benefits a prospective client will receive from your product or service. Value propositions need to be based on research and a strong understanding of your territory or market.

Your employee value proposition is very similar. It provides a solution to attracting, securing, and retaining top talent. The employee value proposition is the set of benefits that employees and prospective employees will receive from being employed by your organisation. It, too, needs research and a strong understanding by your prospective talent pool. Each individual is unique and will value different benefits, but you can also target cohorts so that your employee value proposition will appeal to different groups. You need to gear it toward the groups that you want, be it risk-taking entrepreneurs or millennials.

Your employee value proposition works to attract candidates, increasing the size of the available talent pool in that more people will want to work with you. It will also increase the fit between candidates and your organisation since both parties will have a better idea of what is required and what is being offered. Your employee value proposition will send a clear signal as to the type of company you are, your values, and your promises.

In the securing phase, the more attractive your employee value proposition, the lower the new-hire compensation premium you will have to pay. Candidates who are attracted to your employee value proposition and wish to join your company will ask for less money to leave their current job and join you.

The correlation between pay and your attractiveness as an employer is significant in the hiring phase (securing your candidate) but also applies throughout the employment lifecycle. Money is rarely a long-term motivator, and people rarely leave an employer just for money. However, if the money is high enough, some people will be prepared to tolerate a perceived hostile work environment for a period of time. You must ask yourself if these are the employees you want and if you are truly getting the best from them.

If you do not want to pay a very high premium to hire or retain employees, work on making your employee value proposition more attractive and aligned to the values of your target employees.

Equally if your employee value proposition is unattractive, candidates may still join but they will seek compensation through increased remuneration.

In terms of retaining talent within the organisation, having a strong, authentic employee value proposition improves employee motivation, effort, and retention. People want to keep working with you, they understand the expectations, and they see the value and are aligned to the company mission.

Of key importance to your employee value proposition is both understanding your company culture and being able to express this in compelling and easily understood terms. Hiring needs to be a two-way process. The clearer you are about your company culture and the expectations you have of all your employees, the easier it will be for candidates to make the right decision about joining you. If you do not hire people who fit your organisation's cultural aspirations, you will struggle to maintain the consistent high performance that is so essential to business success. Culture does not mean hiring people who are all the same (apart from being quite probably illegal, it will stifle creativity and growth and ultimately cost your business money). However, it is about hiring people who share common goals that are consistent, such as personal and team success, business growth, and customer service excellence.

Myths and Stories

When examining your company culture, you need to consider both the aspiration and the reality. Honestly facing up to where you fall short of your aspirations is important. These will form part of the myths and stories in your company. If these are not understood and ultimately managed, your culture will never change. The more you expose your potential hires to your organisation

Myths and stories are a critical part of your organisation's culture. They occur naturally but need to be taken seriously. Conscious and consistent effort should be expended to create myths and stories that are congruent with the company you want to be and culture you want to have.

You will also have recruitment myths and stories. You need to listen to these since they will be communicated to potential new hires. If they are not serving you well, you need to invest the necessary time and energy to develop new ones.

(which is a good thing), the more they will hear and the more they will get to know it (warts and all). Hearing about the "real" company and culture needs to be a positive experience for them.

An example of a disconnect might be where your values state that you believe in collaboration and team work, yet you reward a salesperson who gets good personal results at the cost of others' wellbeing. A recruitment-related myth would be telling candidates that you want to ensure that there is a mutual fit, yet deny them free access to talk to existing staff.

In getting to understand your culture and values, you should also consider your company description, vision, and goal statements. Are these congruent with your values? You should identify the behaviour that would be consistent with these goals and values. Test this by considering the behaviours that are most reinforced through your promotion and remuneration practices (especially commission and bonus). Discrepancies here will erode your employee value proposition and ultimately impact your ability to hire the best talent. If you believe in the value but the reality does not match up, be explicit about the value being aspirational and be transparent about the steps you are taking to make it a reality.

There are also external sources where prospective employees can check out your company and validate your employee value proposition. Social media channels are clear. Interestingly, there is quite a bit of chatter about candidates ensuring that their social media footprint represents the person they want to be seen as by a potential employer. In fact, most recruitment agencies will view candidates' social media footprint and encourage them to tidy it up (pictures on Facebook, LinkedIn profile, etc.). There is less written about prospective employees checking out the informal side of an employer via social media, i.e., how you talk to your customers on Twitter, what people say about you on Facebook, etc., but this happens now and will only happen more as time goes by.

Glassdoor is another way to gain insight into how your employees view you as a recruiter and employer. It is a site where employees and past employees leave anonymous feedback on working at the company. This includes what you are like as an employer, what it is like to be interviewed by you, and salary information. It is increasingly used by candidates to learn about the reputation of an organisation based on people who have interacted with it already. It has a lot of "best place to" reports: best place to work, best place to interview, and so on. As an employer, you need to check your Glassdoor profile from time to time. Not only will it tell you how you are doing but it will also give you an idea of what is important to your people (and by extrapolation, your prospective new hires).

Do Something Today

✓ A useful exercise is to do SWOT (strengths, weaknesses, opportunities, and threats) analyses—one for your company as an employer and one for it as a recruiter. Be brutally honest with yourself. Ideally get input from employees. If you recruit a fair amount, try this exercise with two different sets of employees: one set that has been with you less than six months and one that have been with you five to ten years or more. The difference, if there is one, will tell you a great deal.

My Company as an Employer

Strengths	Weaknesses
Looking internally at your company as an employer; list your strengths. Think about this from the point of view of your employees. An example might be that you have a great employee on-site gym.	Here you should list your weaknesses. An example here would be that car parking is challenging near your office.
Opportunities	Threats
When identifying opportunities, it is helpful to take a broader view, looking externally to your organisation. An example here could be that you have the office space to build an employee gym.	Also looking a bit more externally, an example here is that a competitor is relocating to the area.

My Company as a Recruiter

Strengths	Weaknesses
Here you are looking internally at your organisation as a recruiter. An example here is that you have a vibrant and well-visited Facebook page.	You take quite a long time to make hiring decisions, which has led to candidates dropping out.
Opportunities	Threats
An example here is that you know that by investing in the interface you can improve your employee portal.	Your competitor has just upgraded their employee portal and it is really strong, while yours is a bit cumbersome to use.

Benefit to Your Organisation

For your employee value proposition to benefit your organisation, it needs to be consistently aligned across the whole find/attract, select/secure, and join/flourish employee lifecycle.

Find/attract includes:

- **What the prospective candidates experience with your brand, product, or service.** Many will be direct consumers, others will know people who are, and others still will be impacted about what is said in the media and social sites about you.

- **Your company website.** You might not be able to change it, but you should certainly review it and look at what it says and how it says it. If the tone you encounter online is not consistent with your employee value proposition, you will need to find a way to compensate for this when hiring. If you are the business owner, you should review your website to ensure that its content is fully aligned with the employee value proposition.

- **Your career or job portal (or website).** This needs to align with your main website—abrupt changes in tone between these two vehicles can be confusing. You may choose to have a more personal and informal approach on your career site, but it still needs to line up with your core message unless you want to risk sounding false. This is particularly important if you are trying to appeal to certain sectors of the market—if you try too hard, they will spot this and reject you.

Select/secure includes:

- **How people get in touch with you if they are interested in working with you.** Your approach to speculative applications and the demands you place on interested prospective candidates all make a difference.

Many years ago when applying for jobs at my university hiring fair as an arts major in a time of high unemployment, I was pretty dedicated to applying for jobs and willingly filled in application forms regardless of length. A friend of mine who was blessed with a degree in a much scarcer skills market (engineering) refused to apply for anything with an application longer than two sides.

Many companies missed out on his skills.

This has remained an important lesson for me in recruitment.

- **The interview process.** The criticality of getting the interview process right was discussed earlier in the chapter.
- **The hiring manager.** This person is probably the most important element of employee value proposition alignment in the recruitment experience. This applies not just to the one who is intended to be the immediate line manager but any others who are involved in the interview and recruitment process. They need to be prepared, trained, interesting, and, most important, interested.
- **Communication during the process.** Interview invitations and acceptance or rejection letters all need to convey the message and the value proposition.

Join/flourish phase includes:

- **The first day.** Indeed, the first 20 minutes of the first day is all important and can make or break a new hire's connection with the company, colleagues, and the job. The day

There is a classic HR/recruitment joke that sums up the first-day issue perfectly. You die and float up to the pearly gates to be greeted with a choice: entering heaven immediately, or having a quick look round, then popping down to hell to check things out, float back up, and make a one-time decision on location for the rest of eternity.

Curiosity causes you to have a look round both options. You check out heaven, which is lovely and tranquil with people floating around in bliss; you drop down to hell and are invited in to an amazing party, fabulous outfits, drink, food, fun, music, dance—you name it, it's happening. Checking back in you say, "Heaven is lovely, but I'm afraid it is hell for me." You return to hell, knock on the door, and are horrified. People are miserable, it's hot, and everyone is dressed in burning rags. You gasp and ask, "What happened? It wasn't like this yesterday!" The response? "Yesterday we were recruiting. Today we are back to normal."

needs to be planned and orchestrated to the half hour. This does not mean that new hires cannot be left alone; indeed, giving them some alone time is good practice. But they should have specific things to do during this time.

- **Onboarding or induction programme.** This needs to be properly planned and managed. Responsibility can be given to your new hire, but overall accountability needs to lie with their manager.

Other aspects of this phase, all of which need to be fully aligned, include:

- Interactions with colleagues.
- Goal setting and accountability.
- Leadership.
- Learning and development.
- Performance management.
- Reward and recognition.

Chapter Summary

This chapter has focused on culture and attitude that underpins the whole employee lifecycle. Key messages include:

- Build a company-wide culture of recruiting where every manager and employee is a recruiter.
- Invest in training your recruiting managers.
- Be candidate-centric (focusing on the candidate's needs), sell to the candidates (authentic selling, not sales pitching), build relationships, and make fast decisions.
- Think about the change equation and consider where the candidate sits in terms of each element—dissatisfaction with the present, vision of the future, and first practical steps. Consider also their resistance; explore and mitigate this.
- Trust is an important component in successful hiring. When hiring consider the elements of the Trust Equation: credibility, reliability, and intimacy versus self-interest.
- Build processes that mean that you are always recruiting, not just when you are facing a vacancy.
- Understand and develop your employee value proposition.

- Use SWOT (strengths, weaknesses, opportunities, and threats) to evaluate your company as both an employer and a recruiter.

CHAPTER 4

Define and Template

The defining and templating part of the recruitment process is the preparation phase. The more you do here, the better things will go downstream. Make no mistake: Time and effort invested here will definitely save you time and effort at a later stage.

If you hire infrequently, this stage can only be done on a job-by-job basis. Even so, it cannot be skipped. Regardless of how often you hire, your process will be much less time consuming, consistency will improve, and the quality of your hires will go up when you define and template properly.

Decision/Authorisation to Recruit

For larger organisations, it makes sense to have a more formal authorisation-to-recruit process. Below is an example of such an authorisation. The key elements ask about the reason for the vacancy. This provides measurement on your employment effectiveness. Are you promoting people, exiting poor performers, or losing top talent? Also important is the question about exploring alternatives. This tests whether you are being creative in designing your organisation, developing people, and thinking more broadly, rather than simply jumping to hiring a new person. The case for recruitment is also a good business discipline. Is there a case? What are the consequences of non-replacement?

Manager		Department	
Job Title		Current Job Holder (if any)	
Number of Vacancies (same role)		Is the role in your agreed budget?	Yes No
Job Description Available	Yes No	Person Specification Available	Yes No
Status (choose one)	Temporary Permanent Fixed Term Contract	Search	Internal External Both
Reason for Vacancy			
Have all alternative options—development move, flexible working, non-replacement, restructuring, etc.—been explored and found unsuitable?			Yes No
Case for recruitment, including consequences of non-replacement			
Has the recruitment campaign been designed and signed off?			Yes No
Approved by:		(Date)	
Manager			
HR			

These areas (reason, alternatives, business case) are questions you should ask yourself if you are a small company. You may not need a form, but you should still ask the questions.

Defining the Job

Defining the job is a critical but frequently overlooked part of the hiring process. The job description outlines the responsibilities, parameters, and requirements of the position.

Consider the job description alongside a job requirements profile, which will be needed for selection but that you can also use to induct and develop the job holder.

Recommended Practice

Start from the point of the requirements of the organisation (balancing short and long term). It is good practice to have a standard approach to defining jobs, so use a template. This not only ensures you do not leave something out, but also makes it easier for everyone involved in recruitment to immediately find their way round the document.

Include the key dimensions of the role. Try not to cut short this stage—time invested now will save more time in the long run.

Some key questions to ask yourself:

- What is the key purpose of the job?
- How does it fit into the organisation?
- Are there organisational changes planned that impact this job?
- Is there an existing job description?
- What are the outputs required?
- What are the parameters of responsibility in terms of budget, assets, or people?

- What are the legally required qualifications or certifications, if any?
- If you use a job evaluation system or salary benchmarking, has the job been assessed?

While this "define the job" step sounds obvious, it is not always done well or done at all. Getting this part right will give you something against which to judge the candidates and help the decision-making process in terms of both time and quality.

It is also important to focus on the needs of the job rather than what the current (or previous) job holder did. This has a number of benefits. First, it ensures that you align the job to the requirements of the business. Second, job holders inevitably shape the job to their interests and skills. If what they are doing today is used as the sole basis for the job description, you will be building in bias and missing an opportunity to re-establish the role on actual business requirements. Third, the job holder may well have been in the role for a while. If you are looking to promote into the role, it is unlikely that candidates will have all the experience of someone who has been in it for a period of time.

Factors to consider when developing a job description for a salesperson:

- Will they be selling products or services?
- Is it business-to-business or business-to-consumer?
- Who will they be calling on? What level within the organisations? How senior? What size companies?
- How long is the sales cycle? Is this a one-meeting close or a two-year sales cycle with a wide number of decision makers including professional procurement?
- How complex or technical is the solution they are selling? (Think here about whether you might, in fact, be better off

with someone who is a bit less highly technical than you might have thought. The more technically expert the salesperson, the more they are likely to get drawn into telling the prospect all about it, rather than asking questions to facilitate the prospect getting in touch with their own needs and requirements.)

- Will they be selling as part of a team or primarily by themselves? Team-to-team selling is very different from one-to-one selling.
- Is the job focus to grow existing accounts or to generate new business? Will they need to build and nurture long-term relationships, or will the driver be on closing?
- Will they be responsible for the whole process from lead generation to close, or will they take in qualified leads and pass the sale over at a certain point?
- How much cold calling will be involved?
- Will they be office based or home based and travelling?
- How much autonomy will they have? Who will they be reporting to: the sales manager or the business owner?

You will also need to have a clear and well-documented sales process or template in place. If you do not know how sales are made in your organisation, you will struggle to hire. As we have explored (see Chapter 2, "Cost of Error"), the cost of a hiring mistake is very significant. The lack of a clear sales process is a significant factor in new sales hires failing, and it is one element in which you have 100% control.

The Job Description

The first part of the job description should be the job purpose. What is the purpose of the job? It is the summary statement for the job holder and should demonstrate how the job fits into the organisation. What is the core contribution the job holder will be making to the organisation?

An example for a salesperson might be:

To contribute to the growth and success of the company by generating income through the development of a prospecting pipeline and through generating qualified leads and new business sales within the defined territory. To contribute to the achievement of business development targets and sales targets. To onboard new clients and provide client support to increase client satisfaction and retention.

The next part is to define the key accountabilities. These should be specific and cover all the aspects of the role. The above job purpose could be further defined for the salesperson as follows:

- Build and manage a sales pipeline by proactively generating leads with target companies at senior manager/director level. To generate qualified leads, book and attend initial sales meetings.
- Make outbound calls to cold and partially qualified records within the company's target market database. Calling key decision makers from a broad range of industry sectors, you will be responsible for delivery of agreed results: to identify the key pains or issues the prospects are experiencing and booking meetings where appropriate.
- Attend meetings with prospects you have qualified in advance on the phone to discover their business and personal challenges, the budget they are willing and able to

invest to fix their problems, and their decision-making process (who, when, etc.).

- Obtain clear *yes* or *no* decisions at each stage of the sales process.
- Establish account presence and build trust with key contacts within the target market. This should be delivered through a systematic approach to prospecting, referrals, and networking.
- Develop and maintain a prospecting map comprising target companies, known contacts, key roles and use calls, regular client review meetings, referrals, and other prospecting activities to fill in this map to increase selling to these companies.
- Take responsibility for client relationship management primarily for new clients within the first few months with the company—their first sale and first formal review meeting—through regular phone calls and face-to-face meetings. Formally hand over the responsibility for client relationship to the client manager after the first review meeting and support the client manager to ensure an effective handover.
- Maintain the Customer Relationship Management (CRM) system, capturing data and notes from the prospect interactions into the CRM system accurately, including dates for follow-up actions to ensure the sales process is as smooth as possible.
- Achieve your Key Performance Indicators (KPIs) for volume of activity, results achieved, quality of data, conversions, etc. Communicate results and developments to your manager at the required frequency.
- Undertake other reasonable duties and project work as directed by your manager.

The next section of the job description is the job scope. Job scope includes:

- Financial scope of the role, their financial limits, mandates, and so on. What budgets are they directly responsible for meeting? What revenue levels are they responsible for generating?
- Relationships and people responsibility. What key relationships are they responsible for in terms of customers, staff, colleague interactions, and so on? Are they leading internal committees, maintaining client or customer relationships, managing a team of however many people?
- Scope and complexity of the role. How much problem solving must they do? Do solutions they generate typically have precedents, or are those solutions usually novel and groundbreaking?
- Leadership challenges.
- Client contacts. What is the typical number? How simple or complex are these relationships?
- Freedom to act. How much supervision does this person require? How much autonomy do they have?

The final section is concerned with KPIs. These may include:

- **New sales:** Pipeline, number of new clients, value, and profitability.
- **Growth sales:** Share of wallet, growth percentage, number, value, and profitability.
- **Quality of meetings:** Well-qualified prospects, being well-prepared, good meeting notes, and diligent follow-up actions.
- **Productivity:** Balance available time between priorities, with focused, managed time to best effect.

- **Procedure:** Rigorous systems in place, good documentation, and plans up-to-date and followed.
- **Campaign coordination:** Good project management of different pipeline development campaigns.
- **Organisation:** Accurate maintenance of the CRM system and follow ups all booked in.
- **Client liaison:** Regular and timely contact using multiple touch points.
- **Business development:** Clear business growth strategy, customer analysis, and prospecting plan in place and working.
- **Marketing:** Multi-channel marketing strategy developed and implemented.

Specifying the Candidate

Specifying the candidate, or writing a person specification, is a critical element of recruitment preparation. It is important that this is created at the outset of recruitment and not part way through when your judgment may be swayed by a "compelling" candidate.

When writing a person specification, take care to focus on the requirements of the role you are looking to fill and not the current or previous incumbent's skills, knowledge, and interests. If you do not go back to the basics in terms of requirements, you will end up looking for what you have. This will rarely be possible to find, nor is it even desirable. When people have been in a role for a while, it starts to be shaped and moulded to their interests and preferences. This is perfectly natural and quite reasonable, but it is not the only way that the role can be performed. A review of actual requirements and needs is the only way to create a person specification. If you need further convincing, think about how incumbents are currently doing their jobs. If they had to apply for their current job as they were when you hired them into that role, would they have stood a chance of getting it?

Key elements include:

- **Identification of the job:** Current job title, department, division, location.
- **Purpose:** The purpose of the job and how it is to be achieved with its objectives clearly stated and quantified if possible, the duties involved, and the methods by which they are to be carried out.
- **Responsibilities:** Responsibilities for which resources, for whom, and to whom.
- **Relationships:** With whom the job holder will connect.
- **Physical conditions:** Where and how the work is performed along with any potential physical constraints or health risks.
- **Social conditions:** If group work is involved, what social pressures and influences there are along with what types of people will be contacted.
- **Economic conditions:** Salary range, increments, pensions, other benefits, car, relocation expenses.
- **Promotion prospects:** A realistic assessment of the potential for career progression and the opportunity or necessity to transfer to other locations.

Here are some questions to ask yourself when specifying a sales role:

- Who are the people and at what level will the salesperson be calling on?
- How much technical knowledge will the salesperson need to have?

- Will the salesperson be selling products or services?
- What quantity of products or services need to be sold?
- What is the price, and how does this compare to the marketplace?
- Is the selling cycle short or long?
- Does the position require managing and growing existing accounts, generating new business, or both?
- Will the salesperson need to build and develop long-term relationships, or will the main focus be on closing?
- Will the salesperson be responding to qualified leads, or is cold calling and lead generation a major part of the role?
- Will the salesperson be selling primarily alone or as a member of a team?
- Will the salesperson work out of an office or be home based?
- How autonomous is the role, and how much managerial oversight will be provided?
- Is there an opportunity to learn from others doing the same role, or is this the only role of its kind?

A-Players

We hear a great deal about A-Players when it comes to recruitment. Indeed, I use the term in this book alongside the concept of Winners.

A-Players can be defined as the top 10% of the population available for your position, at that compensation level, for your specific role, and within your location. Available does not mean available to you; it means who exists. If you are not searching in the correct ponds, you might not see any A-Players.

Team Fit

I have talked about using vacancies to change your skills mix, particularly with a mid- to long-term view of your capability requirements. Another area that warrants attention is the team mix. Team fit is about filling gaps and taking account of experience levels; it is not about only hiring people who are the same as your current team.

When filling a position in an existing team or function, you need to take into account the team requirements as well. It is important to have a balanced mix of players in a team. Evidence and experience clearly show that diverse teams create better results than homogeneous teams. Within the bounds of ethical and legal best practices, considering diversity in its broadest sense is important when recruiting. Do not fall into the trap of only hiring people with exactly the same educational background, experience, or indeed skills. You will be missing out on a huge amount of talent.

You also want to be recruiting team players. Yes, you want salespeople who are wired to win—but win with colleagues and against the competition. You want them to compete at a healthy level in the spirit of lifting individual and team performance.

You will also want to look at the skills and experience you have within your team and consider what skills you might need in the longer term as well as at the point of hiring.

Putting together a team matrix can help with this. Let's look at the area of team goals (rather than individual objectives) in the short and long term. Consider what you are selling, to whom, and how this might be changing. Do you have new products in development? Do you have aspirations or plans to expand into new geographies? Any new verticals? Are you moving from product to solution selling?

Your next step is to identify the requirements for achieving each of the goals. Having done this, you should consider the attributes required to deliver the requirements, and then who excels where and with what gaps this leaves you. When hiring, build these gaps into your person specification. Some might be nice to have so you take them into account when you have two strong candidates; others might be essential.

Department/ team goals	Requirements to meet goals	Attributes required in team members	Team members who excel in this area	Gaps
• Expand client base into two new verticals	• Proactive prospecting	• Effective cold calling • Successful at obtaining referrals		• No experience of new verticals
• Expand into one new geography	• Proactive prospecting • Builds strategic alliances	• Effective cold calling • Successful at obtaining referrals • Good alliance building		• No experience of chosen new geography
• Grow existing accounts by 15%	• Increase upselling of additional products and services	• Strong questioning skills • Product/ industry knowledge		• Front line staff do not consistently opportunity spot or convert
• Launch new product achieving £xx sales within 12 months	• Proactive prospecting • Strong account selling	• Product/market knowledge • Competitor knowledge • Strong questioning skills		• Little experience across the team in solution selling
• Move to solution selling to address issue with silo product selling	• Find pain/need and address this rather than pitch products • Increase team knowledge of products	• Strong questioning skills • Excellent listening skills • Product/market knowledge • Competitor knowledge		• Currently selling products in silos, thus missing sales opportunities

| • Shorten selling cycles by 25% | • Qualify or disqualify quickly
• Control the selling process
• Eliminate delays, keep track of actions | • Uses criteria to qualify opportunities systematically
• Assertive closing skills
• Strong process skills
• Organised and disciplined | | • Sales cycle too long, forecasted sales dates missed 50% of the time by two months or more |
| • Provide excellent customer service, 96% satisfaction | • Develop relationships
• Establish and maintain contact | • Excellent people skills
• Organised and disciplined | | • Current satisfaction rate is 80% with range from 43% to 98% |

I am an advocate of hiring high performers—people who strive to be the best that they can be. This does not mean that everyone needs to be ambitious for organisational progression. If they are ambitious to perform well, a healthy mix of people at different stages of their careers and ambitions works well. If everyone wants to be promoted, you will struggle to meet all these aspirations and will end up losing some of your top talent. If some of the people on your team want to perform well but not put in extra hours and not strive for a promotion, this works in a mix with others who are striving to progress. Taking a lifecycle view of your employees is important if you want to be able to hire and retain talent. If you recognise that at different points in different people's lives they will have different priorities and accept that this does not mean that they are not dedicated to doing an excellent job, you will be able to build strong, high-performing teams.

It is important therefore, to not confuse high performance with high potential. It is also important to be able to define high performance for every role within your organisation. If you cannot describe it, your people will not achieve it. High performance is about the current role. In fact, confusing the two is one of the reasons so many people get over-promoted. Have you ever turned your best salesperson into the sales manager and found that you have lost your best salesperson (negatively impacted sales by losing theirs) and introduced your worst sales manager (negatively impacting sales by damaging the whole sales team)? The best at one job is not necessarily the best at another.

Do Something Today

✓ Take a piece of paper and write down four headings: poor performance, mediocre performance, good performance, and high performance. Then write down five descriptors under each heading.

✓ Ask a peer (a colleague with the same job) or your manager (if you don't have a peer) to do the same. This will validate your opinions and also tell you if the management standards are uniform.

Hiring Executives

From time to time it is necessary to hire at the top of an organisation. Either because your succession plans have broken down or you want to take the business in a different direction or move it forward at a different pace, you want to disrupt the current processes, culture, and way of doing things. These are tricky appointments, as you will recall from Chapter 2, and the cost of error can be high if not catastrophic if you get this appointment wrong. Where possible, organisations can mitigate their risk by hiring into one of the C-suite roles with the intention of making the ultimate appointment to CEO or company president within 12 months.

When hiring externally for the top role you need to be very clear what you are wanting from the new hire. Is the requirement to disrupt and change, to aggressively grow, or to stabilise the share price and settle the analysts? Or something else? Getting this purpose fully understood is critical to the success of the hire. Getting it wrong will be costly.

Looking at the following list of the characteristics of entre-preneurial leaders provides a useful illustration of this. If you are looking for change and you have a board or owner that are able to delegate and willing to take risks (and have the ability to manage risk in its organisational leader), then these will be characteristics to look for.

- High need for achievement.
- A belief in the ability to control the environment through their own actions (internal locus of control).
- Risk taking: a comfort with and enjoyment of risk.
- Innovativeness and problem-solving capabilities.
- Acceptance of responsibility.
- Organisation: personally well-organised and able to bring together components of a venture (including people).
- Hard work and energy.
- Optimism: the belief that anything is possible.
- Orientation to excellence.
- Profit orientation (serving as a meter to gauge success and achievement).
- Reward orientation (recognition and respect as much as money).
- Charismatic, compelling, driven.

If however the organisational context will not allow for the levels of autonomy, achievement, or risk, etc., your hire will quickly become ineffective and in turn frustrated. This will in turn lead to them being disruptive or leaving, neither of which is an acceptable outcome and both of which will damage the profits, staff, and reputation of the organisation.

When hiring for the top position, the recognition of fit is important—fit with the vision and strategy for the organisation and fit with the board/owner's operating model.

Interestingly, with very senior hires, the ability to hire from different industries or sectors can be easier than for more operational roles. There will be some exceptions to this, but when hiring to the C-suite you can afford to be creative in terms of sourcing. You must, however, be much more rigorous in terms of referencing. While top performers will want to see opportunities for stretch and growth before accepting a role, I would suggest that it is too great a risk to hire someone who has not operated at the top of an organisation as an external hire to the top of your organisation. They can have been top of an autonomous division or a smaller company, but learning the role at the same time as learning the company is less than desirable.

Planning for C-suite hires becomes even more critical since you may want, as mentioned above, to pull them into the organisation via a stepping stone role.

The focus in this segment has been the top role, but many of the principles apply equally to any C-suite hire. You will, however, have a bit more latitude around promoting when hiring, provided they have a strong match in terms of attitude, competency, and competence.

Hiring Inexperienced Salespeople

I want to take a moment to explore the pros and cons of hiring inexperienced salespeople. To put my cards straight on the table, I am a fan of doing this. But to give a slightly more balanced view, here are some considerations.

Pros of Inexperienced Salespeople

- **Open-minded.** They are going to be open-minded and can be trained in your way. They do not have any preconceived ideas about the baggage that goes with the selling profession. Indeed, if you start them well, they can be quite fearless with cold calling or walk-ins. They simply don't know to be afraid (provided you hire people with a healthy self-esteem).

- **Competitive.** Chances are that they will have experience being competitive—sports, school scores, etc. If they have tasted the thrill of winning, sales can become a new avenue to capture that same feeling.

- **Balance.** A blend of inexperienced and experienced team members can make good sense depending on your marketplace. Less experienced salespeople can call on some of the lower-value accounts and spend more time prospecting new accounts. The more experienced can channel their energy in major accounts and building relationships. Wisdom balances enthusiasm.

- **No bad habits.** Inexperienced salespeople arrive with a clean slate—or as clean as anyone can have. You can therefore start them off the way you want and train them in both technique and good habits.

- **Eager to learn.** Assuming effective hiring, they will be receptive to new ideas and eager to learn. There will not be any, "We don't do things that way around here."

Cons of Inexperienced Salespeople

- **Inexperienced.** Makes sense, right? You will have to bear the cost and time of training them—not just in sales but, if they have limited work experience as well, in the way the business world works. They might not know enough to refuse to accept prospect stalls and objections simply because they don't know any better.
- **A lot of capability but little ability.** Recent graduates especially quite simply have not learned to work or operate in a business setting. With some, this can result in somewhat pushy or arrogant behaviour.
- **Immature.** This could manifest itself in blaming others rather than taking responsibility, i.e., the problem was the buyer (never going to buy anyway), the price (competitor is cheaper), or the manager (should have supported them more) rather than their own responsibility.
- **Lack of gravitas.** They may have less gravitas and less influence with prospects and clients.
- **Turnover.** They might leave.

If you are going to hire inexperienced salespeople, particularly those who have never worked before, consider the following:

- You will need to develop a hiring competence checklist that enables you to spot potential. They won't have much of a track record for you to rely on. Potential spotting is best achieved through a mixed selection process, psychometrics, assessment centre exercises, and interviewing.

Essentially, you need to look for the competencies that will provide the building blocks for success.

- Ideally you need to recruit in cohorts—groups of three to eight at a time. This fits the university "recruitment fair" approach. There are two reasons for this. One is simply cost and efficiency. You will need to provide considerable training for inexperienced hires, and it is more efficient to do this in groups. The other is that they will grow and perform better if they have peers. There will be some healthy competition, you will have better benchmarks, and they will have some protection from the traditional cynicism of the experienced salesperson.

- You will need to consider if your industry sector and target clients will be suitable for the inexperienced. If you require heavy prospecting and lead generation activity, and have the opportunity to sell to smaller accounts at lower values (either because this is your product or service or because you have a range and they can start at the bottom end), then you may well be able to accommodate and benefit from inexperienced salespeople. If there are only 50 companies in your target client base and the sales take a long time with each step open to failure, you might not want to experiment with a newbie.

Whether hiring inexperienced or experienced salespeople, if you are hiring for sales and other customer-facing roles you need to be prepared to invest in training. The sooner you start the training the better.

Question: What if I spend money training them and they leave?
Answer: What if you don't train them and they stay?

Hiring Millennials

People born between 1980 and 2000 have been dubbed Millennials. This group is a topic of conversation across most businesses today. In 2015, a tipping point in the United States was reached in which Millennials outnumbered the previous generation in the workforce. It therefore is important to understand them and be effective at hiring and retaining them.

Philosophically, there is considerable debate about the accuracy of isolating groups of people generationally. There is also a great danger of stereotyping people, which is potentially libelous as well. Therefore, when talking about and to your workforce, I would definitely avoid the label. Nevertheless, there are certain

"Anything that is in the world when you're born is normal and ordinary and just a natural part of the way the world works. Anything that's invented between when you're fifteen and thirty-five is new and exciting and revolutionary and you can probably get a career in it. Anything invented after you're thirty-five is against the natural order of things." —Douglas Adams, as quoted in *Disruptive Technologies: Understand, Evaluate, Respond,* by Paul Armstrong (Kogan Page, 2017).

"The companies that want to attract the top Millennial talent will have to engage and train employees for a short, two- to five-year learning journey (and then help them find their next great opportunity). They will have to understand and accept that no one wants to stay at one company forever. Employers can think of their employees as not just independent contractors, but as dynamic individuals with long-term career and personal ambitions. If they help someone move on to do something even better, that former employee will continue to have brand loyalty and may even recommend their friend for the job they just left. It's going to be a much more fluid system of sharing and investing in talent." —Adam Poswolsky, as quoted in *Disruptive Technologies: Understand, Evaluate, Respond*, by Paul Armstrong (Kogan Page, 2017)

implications for hiring and employment practices that you will need to master if you are going to attract and retain a high performing workforce in the future. Understanding Millennials will be critical to your future success.

A few additional comments:

- Every generation is uncomfortable with the next generation. Millennials are not better or worse; they just are.
- Millennials have grown up with technology and are more comfortable with it than previous generations. Through technology, they are highly connected with the outside world and other people. This connectedness gives them

more benchmarks and more choice in terms of employment than any previous generation. They can and will
compare you to other employers, and they can and will
tell people about this and share better opportunities with
their connections.

- Millennials are probably the most diverse group of people
in your company.

- Millennials are the first generation that grew up with the
internet as standard. Paul Armstrong writes: "Open source,
collaboration, [and] unlimited knowledge and access has
been a 'right' for this group since they were old enough to
know what a keyboard is" (from *Disruptive Technologies:
Understand, Evaluate, Respond*, 2017).

There are implications in terms of the hiring and employment
of Millennials that need to be understood and incorporated into
your employee value proposition, candidate attraction strategies,
work design, and employment.

- When hiring, make use of the Millennial's affinity for networking. This opens up geographies and sectors that previously were hard to reach. Make use of their connections
and encourage introductions to the company and referrals
for filling vacancies.

- Harness the Millennial's connections in creating and
keeping alive alumni groups. This is going to be a much
more mobile workforce, and you need to accept that they
will leave. Change your paradigm so that you start to work
with their idea of a career (multiple companies, geographies, and roles). If you do this well, they will become
advocates and a source of future hires, and in addition they

may come back themselves. Keeping in touch with former employees will be critical.

- Let them take charge. In terms of hiring, areas such as talent pools, alumni groups, and strategic university relationships can be better managed by this group than centralised in the HR department. Yes, this will lead to a loss of control, but it will also result in better connections and better access to talent.

- Think about your hiring timescales. Expectations of speed get higher from generation to generation, and Millennials want this faster than ever. If your processes are slow or the gaps between action or communication too long, your prospective Millennial will lose motivation and commitment. This applies to hiring as well as working. This also ties to the section on technology in Chapter 5 ("Finding: Efficient, Effective, and Creative Sourcing"). Applications need to be responded to instantly (this is their experience of technology and anything different will jar), bureaucracy needs to be removed ("Cover letter? Why not an email, or better still where do I load my CV?"), the process needs to make sense and be transparent, and they need to be given the opportunity to check you out as much as you are checking them out.

- Avoid prolonged, one-way hiring processes. Mix it up a bit. Use workshops, visit days, and less formal discussions alongside the formal interview to get to know candidates and let them get to know you.

- Don't stick too rigidly to past expectations about career path and CVs. Millennials may well have moved around more, many are likely to have been made redundant (if this ever was a suggestion of mediocrity it can no longer be so), and some won't have the right experience at all after having struggled to break into the mainstream job market. Base your hiring a bit more on attitude, competencies, and potential, and then train them. This requires much more sophisticated selection skills so you may need to train your hiring managers as well.

- You will need to be more transparent and congruent (as outlined in Chapter 3, "Employee Value Proposition" section) if you are to attract and retain Millennials. Think about how you can achieve this during the hiring experience.

- Commit to their training. Millennials want to learn. When they stop learning, they will likely move on. When hiring, talk about training, development, stretch, and challenge (and then ensure that this is the reality of their work experience). Be ready to break current myths about how long it takes before someone should be allowed to do something. Training should be interactive, real, ongoing, reinforced, and not one-off, off site, and with the trainer in transmit only mode.

- A more open mindset and systems need to be developed to handle the innovation and new ways of doing things. If you let Millennials contribute, not only will you benefit from the innovativeness but you will also engage and satisfy them for longer.

- Think more flexibly around job design and organisation structure. Millennials may well be the first generation to really embrace teamwork and diversity. These things will come more naturally to them. Look at some of your systems, including rewards, and see if they optimise the Millennial's motivation and contribution.

- Continue to set clear goals with timescales and clear

performance expectations. Everyone performs better with goals and needs to know what is expected of them. Focus more on the output or result when defining expectations.

- Approach working time more flexibly. You may need to consider radical flexible working (not just the option to start at 9:30 A.M.) and part-time. Clearly business needs must come first. If you require cover, you will need to set cover hours—but perhaps let the team work out how they are going to do it. Ask yourself, "Do I need my salespeople to be in the office from 8:30 A.M. to 5:30 P.M., or do I need them to make 50 calls and two prospect visits a day?"

- Improve your management skills and your accountability processes. If you are going to provide a freer working environment, it requires different leadership skills. Give feedback; ask for it as well. Millennials want to feel they are making progress and need lots of feedback to be able to grow and develop.

- Don't try to shut down their social media. It won't work, and it will harm your employment relationship. Harness this for your hiring attraction and brand marketing. Coach those who cannot find the right balance and ultimately impose consequences if it leads to poor performance, but do not constrain the whole group simply because a few don't get it. If you try, they will simply find an alternative employer who is more open-minded about social media.

- Build challenge and change into roles.

- Demonstrate that they are being heard and understood. Wanting to be heard and understood is the natural human condition, but Millennials see that this is their right as well as their desire. Deny them this right at your peril.

- Millennials want to enjoy being at work. This does not mean that they do not want to work hard (some do, some don't), but they do want to enjoy themselves. In the Maslow hierarchy of needs, they are usually beyond hygiene and security and at social/belonging and esteem levels, striving for self-actualisation.

Looking at the above list, there is very little that is not covered elsewhere in the book. When it comes to Millennials, the trick is to be more explicit about the intent and a bit more courageous with the implementation.

SEARCH

The acronym SEARCH will help you identify and organise the attributes you require.

- **Skills:** What specific skills must successful candidates possess?
- **Experience:** What specific activities, types of clients, areas of responsibility, work history, and background factors are relevant to the job under consideration?
- **Attitudes:** How do the candidates approach work, colleagues, and life? What guiding principles should successful candidates possess?
- **Results:** What success have candidates had in the past? What results have been produced in similar situations? Have these individuals outperformed others in a similar situation?
- **Cognitive skills:** What is their ability to learn the information and processes necessary to do the job well? What is the candidates' ability to think and learn relative to the demands of the job?
- **Habits:** What specific behaviours and approaches to

accomplishing life tasks and getting work done are necessary for the successful candidates in this position?

Skills

Skills refer to specific knowledge and ability required to successfully perform the functions of a position. These may be technical or non-technical.

Technical skills will require different levels of competence.
For example:

- Ability to use a specific CRM system.
- Ability to use spreadsheets as a day-to-day work tool.
- Ability to use advanced spreadsheets including macros and
  complex multi-sheet functionality.

Some technical skills can be identified through professional
qualification—accounting, legal, HR, computing—verified by
certificates. Always verify any qualification or certificate that you
require for the role. Do not simply take the word of the candidate
or assume if it is in the CV it must be true.

Every summer, Britain's Higher Education Degree
Datacheck (HEDD) surveys students and graduates
about degree fraud. The annual results are pretty consistent—about a third of people embellish or exaggerate
their academic qualifications when applying for jobs.
It's also consistent when matched with other surveys
in the United Kingdom, the United States, and in
other countries.

Where specific technical skills are required for a role, you should build into your interview programme a test for these. Chapter 6, "Inventorying," talks more about this.

Non-technical skills might include the ability to communicate verbally and in written form. Some skills are essential and some are nice to have. You should be clear when creating your person specification on which is which.

You can test for verbal communication on a phone interview or during a face-to-face interview. Written communication is trickier. While some negative indicators are very clear, i.e., typos, grammatical errors, etc., or the converse, namely a well-written CV, cannot be taken as proof of writing skills. These days it is easy and not costly to have your CV written or reviewed by a professional CV writer. The quality of a CV can therefore no longer be taken as proof of competence.

Examples of skills for sales roles include:

- Ability to approach and engage others face-to-face and on the phone.
- Ability to demonstrate hearing and understanding and laser-focused listening.
- Ability to analyse situations and problem solve.
- Ability to present ideas clearly.
- Ability to address and facilitate prospects' overcoming their stalls and objections.
- Ability to bring a sale to closure.
- Ability to lead/manage a sales team.

Experience

Experience refers to having performed the type of work you are hiring for and assumed the level of responsibilities or challenges.

>   Avoid defining experience in terms of years, i.e., "five
> years in an outside sales role." Apart from the legal ram-
> ifications (it puts you at risk of age discrimination in
> some countries such as the UK), it is meaningless. Five
> years selling the same low-value product to a captive
> audience is not the same as two years selling solutions
> into a challenging market. Even if you are looking for a
> salesperson to sell low value into a captive market, why
> five years? Why not four, or three, or six?

Previous experience does not guarantee success, but it can help. Having experience with team selling or long sales cycles would be examples. When considering experience, it can be helpful to draw out transferable skills/knowledge. So, complex selling over a two-year cycle involves a number of elements that would be immediately transferable to you. On the other hand, selling contracts into government agencies that involved a number of levels of tendering might not be relevant if you sell directly into the private sector (although you might still find some transferable skills—you would have to ask how much of what you don't want might also get transferred).

Experience is not about the number of years someone has done something; it is about what they have actually done and learned.

Examples of experience for sales roles include:

- Selling high-value products/services.
- Enterprise selling with long sales cycles.
- Developing new markets through cold calling.
- Developing goals and sales targets.

- Selling to C-suite executives.
- Selling into professional service firms.

Attitude

Attitude refers to the state of mind the candidate must have in order to perform effectively in the role. Being open to input and being willing to learn and try new approaches are examples. Unlike experience, which focus on what candidates have done, attitude is about how the candidates relate to the experience and their beliefs. Chapter 6 talks about the attitude of Winners; it is these attitudes you are seeking when hiring.

Examples of attitude for sales roles include being:

- Approachable and warm.
- Self-confident and assertive (not aggressive).
- Open to change.
- Oriented strongly toward self-development.
- Emotionally under control.
- Willing to take responsibility.

Results

Results refer to the accomplishments that verify the candidate's ability to apply knowledge and skills. They tend to be the outputs achieved. Growing a territory and generating a certain number of sales are examples. When looking for evidence of results during the selection process, care needs to be taken to establish the precise role candidates played in achieving the results. Also, how much did they initiate vs. simply doing as they were told? How lucky were they?

Examples of results for sales roles include:
- Concrete examples of meeting and exceeding targets.
- Opening a new territory.

- Selling a new product.
- Earning top salesperson position.
- Having a track record of growing accounts.

Cognitive Skills

Analytical thinking and business judgment would be examples of cognitive skills. In a broader sense, this also includes an individual's knowledge about the product, marketplace, and industry and the ability to appropriately apply that knowledge to the requirements of the position.

Examples of cognitive skills for sales roles include:

- Being a fast learner.
- Demonstrating product and market knowledge.
- Being able to think on one's feet.
- Understanding human behaviour.
- Using a systematic approach to analyse business opportunities.
- Absorbing, analysing, and summarising complex information.

Habits

Habits are those things candidates do unconsciously, without thinking. Within habits, you would also add the competencies you are seeking. Competencies are predispositions to behave in ways associated with superior performance or success. We will look at competencies in more detail later.

Examples of habits for sales roles include:

- Being goal oriented.
- Being structured and organised.
- Having time competency—ability to manage time and resources.

- Staying calm under pressure.
- Tracking behaviours, activities, and results.

Habits or competencies are critical in hiring and equally important in evaluating potential. Many are trainable, but some are harder to train than others.

Developing the list of competencies associated with superior performance in a role is an important part of templating your recruitment. Once you know what you are looking for, you can then go about finding it in your potential hires.

The interview guide in Chapter 6 ("Interviewing") has examples of competencies and the questions you can ask to discover if candidates have them at the required level.

Examples of SEARCH

Below you will find four SEARCH profiles: a C-suite executive, the hunter sales role, the account manager role, and the sales manager role. They will need to be adjusted to suit your specific jobs, context, products, or services, but are illustrative and a good place to start.

C-Suite Executive Role

SKILLS Specific knowledge and abilities required by the position	• Leadership. • Dealing with analysts, shareholders, and other stakeholders. • Presenting and negotiating skills. • Resilient and able to balance competing demands and priorities and stay in control. • Innovativeness and problem-solving capabilities. • Able to be an ambassador for the company. • Strategy development and implementation. • Able to be trusted and respected by internal and external stakeholders. • Question intelligently, debate constructively, challenge rigorously, and decide dispassionately.

EXPERIENCE Performed the type of work, delivered the responsibility, and applied the knowledge required by position	• Track record of managing a P&L with a high degree of autonomy. • Leadership and management of a senior team. • Demonstrated experience at board level. • Governance experience: implementing and operating the systems and processes concerned with ensuring the overall direction, effectiveness, supervision, and accountability of an organisation.
ATTITUDE State of mind of the candidate	• High need for achievement. • A belief in the ability to control the environment through their own actions (internal locus of control). • Takes responsibility. • Optimistic and abundance mentality. • Orientation to excellence. • Profit orientation. • Strong desire to learn.
RESULTS Accomplishments that verify one's ability	• Track record of delivery and achievement that can be clearly attributable to their efforts (direct and through leadership of others). • Strong network of influencers. • The reputation, stature, and authority to command immediate respect both externally and internally. • The confidence and courage to stand "firm under fire" and to shape rather than be shaped by external events.
COGNITIVE SKILLS Ability to learn/ process information required by the job	• Fast learner. • Conceptual thinking. • Analytical thinking. • Strategic thinking. • Good understanding of the role of an executive officer.
HABITS Specific behaviours and actions required of the job and linked to superior performance	• Strong work ethic. • Self-disciplined and structured. • Goal focused, short and long term. • Meets commitments—to others and self. • Holds self accountable. • Strong self development motivation, humble enough to learn. • Networks effectively.

Hunter Sales Role

This role has a strong focus on acquiring new sales by hunting for new prospects and clients and chasing new leads. This may be for short or long sales cycles and includes prospecting (finding and getting in front of potential prospects) as well as selling and closing. It may or may not include growing opportunities or accounts. The hunter is driven to take action and close sales as fast as possible, and sales quantity is important to them.

SKILLS Specific knowledge and abilities required by the position	• Prospecting for new business. • Core selling skills: communication (oral and written), laser-focused listening, questioning, and probing, qualifying competency, finding pain, building parity-based rapport, ability to learn. • Effective and compelling telephone approach. • Consultative, relationship selling. • Presenting. • Negotiation. • Account planning. • Accurate sales forecasting. • Works well with others, demonstrates teamwork, seeks/is able to understand and meet clients' needs and find solutions. • Perseverance and the ability to respectfully challenge customers' answers. • Well-organised and thorough, even under pressure. • Enjoys working within a target-driven team environment.
EXPERIENCE Performed the type of work, delivered the responsibility, and applied the knowledge required by position	• Track record of selling complex solutions/product/software systems (etc., as relevant). • Growing a territory and existing accounts through referrals. • Navigating long sales cycles. • Commission based selling. • Team-selling experience and track record. • Proven successful track record in a target-driven outbound sales environment. • Experience of selling solutions in business-to-business markets. • Experience of selling to prospects at all levels including top level (C-suite), professional buyers and multiple decision makers. • Relevant business experience. • Skilled at multi-tasking and prioritising, particularly under tight deadlines. • Creating and implementing a personal sales plan. • Cold calling to get appointments.
ATTITUDE State of mind of the candidate	• Self-motivated, strong desire to win. • Gets a kick out of making sales coupled with strong determination to make sales. • Drives to the close. • Takes personal responsibility. • Strong self-development orientation. • Strong prospecting orientation. • Perseverance and tenacity. • "Can do" attitude—does what it takes. • Results orientation. • Customer-service orientation. • Goal oriented. • Positive. • Confident. • Assertive. • Attitude of abundance. • Sense of urgency.

RESULTS Accomplishments that verify one's ability	• Track record of finding and securing new clients. • Spots issues and problems and works to resolve them. • Generates client satisfaction and loyalty. • High client retention. • Able to get through obstacles and in front of decision makers. • Grows accounts, generates business from existing clients. • Examples of building a territory from scratch or launching a new product/service. • Received referrals and testimonials. • Meets or exceeds goals.
COGNITIVE SKILLS Ability to learn/process information required by the job	• Able to process client requirements into solutions. • Innovative. • Problem solving. • Analytical thinking. • Conceptual thinking. • Strategic thinking. • Spots opportunities. • Makes connections. • Quick to learn new concepts and approaches. • Flexibility, adaptability, and quick thinking; the ability to quickly absorb information about prospect's company.
HABITS Specific behaviours and actions required of the job and linked to superior performance	• Strong work ethic. • Organised and systematic. • Self-disciplined and structured. • Goal focused; sets daily, weekly, monthly, and annual goals. • Meets commitments—to others and self. • Holds self accountable. • Seeks feedback and learns from experience. • Pre-meeting preparation and post-meeting review. • Seeks referrals. • Networks effectively. • Works well with others, demonstrates teamwork, seeks to understand and meet clients' needs and find solutions. • Good focus on the detail of presentation and quality of information. • Has the drive and determination to make things happen.

Account Manager Role

The focus here is retaining and growing accounts and getting more business from existing clients. It requires long-term relationship building based on mutual understanding and respect. The ability to set, manage, and meet expectations is critical. This is more of a farmer sales role. Farmers focus on developing long-term customer relationships and working with others. The quality of the relationship and building loyalty is important to them.

SKILLS Specific knowledge and abilities required by the position	• Managing account relationships. • Core skills: communication (oral and written), laser-focused listening, questioning, and probing, qualifying competency, finding pain, building parity-based rapport, ability to learn. • Presenting. • Effective and compelling telephone approach. • Negotiation. • Consultative, relationship selling. • Strategic account planning. • Accurate account forecasting. • Works well with others, demonstrates teamwork, seeks/is able to understand and meet clients' needs and find solutions. • Perseverance and the ability to respectfully challenge customers' answers. • Well-organised and thorough, even under pressure. • Enjoys working within a target-driven team environment. • Territory management.
EXPERIENCE Performed the type of work, assumed the responsibility, and applied the knowledge required by position	• Growing accounts. • Relevant business experience. • Track record of managing complex accounts with multiple stakeholders. • Effectively dealing with top decision makers and multiple decision makers. • Growing a territory and existing accounts through referrals. • Navigating long sales cycles. • Team-selling experience and track record. • Proven successful track record in a target-driven outbound sales environment. • Experience of selling solutions in business-to-business markets. • Experience of selling to prospects at all levels. • Skilled at multi-tasking and prioritising, particularly under tight deadlines. • Creating and implementing a personal account management plan.
ATTITUDE State of mind of the candidate	• Gets a kick out of retaining and growing accounts coupled with strong determination to achieve both. • Takes personal responsibility. • Strong self-development orientation. • Self-motivating. • Strong prospecting orientation. • Perseverance and tenacity. • "Can do" attitude—does what it takes. • Results orientation. • Customer-service orientation. • Client focused. • Drive to delight. • Goal oriented. • Positive. • Confident. • Assertive. • Attitude of abundance. • Sense of urgency.

RESULTS Accomplishments that verify one's ability	• Spots issues and problems and works to resolve them. • Generates client satisfaction and loyalty. • High client retention. • Grows accounts, generates business from existing clients. • Examples of building a territory from scratch or launching a new product/service. • Received referrals and testimonials.
COGNITIVE SKILLS Ability to learn/process information required by the job	• Innovative. • Problem solving. • Analytical thinking. • Conceptual thinking. • Strategic thinking. • Spots opportunities. • Makes connections. • Quick to learn new concepts and approaches. • Flexibility, adaptability, and quick thinking; the ability to quickly absorb information about prospect's company.
HABITS Specific behaviours and actions required of the job and linked to superior performance	• Strong work ethic. • Organised and systematic. • Self-disciplined and structured. • Goal focused; sets daily, weekly, monthly, and annual goals. • Meets commitments—to others and self. • Holds self accountable. • Seeks feedback and learns from experience. • Pre-meeting preparation and post-meeting review. • Seeks referrals. • Networks effectively. • Works well with others, demonstrates teamwork, seeks to understand and meet clients' needs and find solutions. • Good focus on the detail of presentation and quality of information. • Has the drive and determination to make things happen.

Sales Manager Role

This section looks more at the management side of things. If a sales manager is also responsible for selling, those requirements will be found in the above examples.

SKILLS Specific knowledge and abilities required by the position	• Holding individuals accountable. • Coaching. • Mentoring. • Supervising. • Resolving conflicts. • Setting targets and objectives. • Questioning. • Hiring, interviewing, and selecting talent. • Facilitating. • Negotiating. • Organising others' work and plans. • Setting direction. • Visioning and inspiring. • Leading, including through change. • Retaining and rewarding talent.
EXPERIENCE Performed the type of work, assumed the responsibility, and applied the knowledge required by position	• Track record of managing a team of salespeople with improved sales performance year-on-year. • Examples of leading high-performance teams. • Managing commission-based sales teams. • Relevant business and industry experience. • Experience of selling complex solutions with short and long sales cycles. • Leading team selling. • Examples of leading change.
ATTITUDE State of mind of the candidate	• Takes personal responsibility. • Strong self-development orientation. • Self-motivating. • Results orientation. • Drive to delight. • Goal oriented. • Positive. • Confident. • Assertive. • Attitude of abundance. • Sense of urgency. • Comfortable with ambiguity. • Embraces change.
RESULTS Accomplishments that verify one's ability	• Teams achieve closing rates of x% or greater. • Teams achieve retention rates of x% or greater. • Examples of team members being developed and promoted from within. • Consistent selling and account growth from all team members. • Ability to hire, onboard, and retain top talent.

COGNITIVE SKILLS Ability to learn/process information required by the job	· Innovative. · Problem solving. · Analytical thinking. · Conceptual thinking. · Strategic thinking. · Spots opportunities. · Makes connections. · Quick to learn new concepts and approaches. · Flexibility, adaptability, and quick thinking; the ability to quickly absorb information about a prospect's company. · Commercially minded.
HABITS Specific behaviours and actions required of the job and linked to superior performance	· Collaborative, takes people with them. · Strong work ethic. · Organised and systematic. · Self-disciplined and structured. · Goal focused; sets daily, weekly, monthly, and annual goals. · Meets commitments—to others and self. · Holds self accountable. · Seeks feedback and learns from experience. · Pre-meeting preparation and post-meeting review. · Seeks referrals. · Networks effectively. · Works well with others, demonstrates teamwork, seeks to understand and meet clients' needs and find solutions. · Good focus on the detail of presentation and quality of information. · Has the drive and determination to make things happen.

Templating

Creating standard templates for everything you do is an important part of effective recruitment. You want to deploy your thinking and creativity with the candidate and in the selection decision. The more effective and efficient the processes you follow, the more time and attention you can give to the other aspects of the recruiting and hiring.

In terms of templates, you should have the following in place:

- Job description templates for all your roles.
- Person specifications for all your roles.
- Job advertisement templates and examples.

- Additional information for candidates—ideally on your hiring portal and online presence (website, Facebook, LinkedIn, etc.).
- Standard email text for confirming the phone interview, face-to-face interview, invitation to take psychometric tests, turndowns, etc.
- Hiring manager interview template.

Example Role Profile

By way of providing some illustrations, two example role profiles have been included: one for a non-executive director, and one for an inside sales executive.

Role title: Non-Executive Director
Role Purpose: To be a full member of the board and provide entrepreneurial leadership, within a framework of effective and prudent controls that enable risk to be assessed and managed and sustainable value to be created. To help create an environment in which effective challenge of the executive is expected and achieved in the boardroom before decisions are taken on major risk and strategic issues. To make an informed and critical contribution.

Key Accountabilities
1. Contribute fully to the business of the board, taking full account of the issues and the concerns of all board members and the interests of the staff and shareholders. 2. Keep under review the general progress and long-term development of the company. Identify and monitor key business, financial, and reputational risks and controls and provide effective oversight of performance delivery. 3. Constructively challenge and help develop proposals on strategy. 4. Promote the highest standards of corporate governance, seeking compliance with the provisions of relevant codes of practice and legislation. 5. Ensure that individual business decisions conform to agreed strategies and policies. 6. Ensure that the company does everything that is required of it by law and regulation. 7. Scrutinise the performance of management in meeting agreed goals and objectives and monitor the reporting of performance. 8. Participate in the ongoing monitoring and annual evaluation of the performance of the CEO/president. Hold the CEO/president and the subordinate team accountable for the execution and delivery of company performance against agreed business plans and key strategic goals. 9. Diligently carry out the duties and responsibilities required by legislation and service agreement. 10. Chair or be a member of the board committees as required.

Financial Scope (limits/mandates, etc.)	People Responsibility (customers/staff, etc.)
Company Revenue: £xx,xxx Number of employees: xx	Work effectively within the board. Build and maintain relationships with the executive team and external stakeholders.

Expectations, knowledge, skills, qualifications, and experience

Expectations of the Non-Executive Director
- Uphold the highest standards of integrity and probity.
- Contribute to the style and tone of board discussions to promote effective decision making and constructive debate; promote effective relationships and open communication, both inside and outside the boardroom, between non-executive directors and the executive team.
- Monitor to ensure effective implementation of board decisions.
- Represent the board internally and externally and, in conjunction with the CEO/president develop the group's corporate communications policy.
- Be perceived as independent and meet the independence criteria set out in relevant codes of practice or legislation.
- Exercise reasonable skill and care in carrying out their duties commensurate with their knowledge and experience, having regard for employees and external stakeholders.
- Build a constructive relationship with the executive directors and other key staff and, where appropriate, an effective relationship with the company's external auditors and other advisors.

Essential skills, knowledge, and experience
- Proven track record as non-executive within a similarly sized and complex organisation.
- Good understanding of the role of a non-executive director and able to operate effectively in such a role at the highest level.
- Good understanding and experience of boardroom and corporate governance issues.
- Deep and broad relationships, both in the business and stakeholder communities.
- The reputation, stature, and authority to command immediate respect both externally and internally.
- The confidence and courage to stand "firm under fire" and to shape rather than be shaped by external events.
- A practical, pragmatic, and informal style and an effective questioner and listener.

Key competencies and behaviours
- A respected ambassador for the company.
- Committed to maximising long-term shareholder value.
- Help shape company strategy.
- Demonstrate independence of judgment.
- Question intelligently, debate constructively, challenge rigorously, and decide dispassionately.
- Has the trust and respect of other members of the board and senior executive team.
- Effective member of the board team.
- Communicating complex messages succinctly.
- Collaborating across boundaries.

Committee Roles

Chair
Manage the business of the committee and set its agenda, taking full account of the issues and the concerns of all board members and the interests of the staff and shareholders. Ensure that the agenda strikes the right balance between short- and long-term issues.

Committee Members
Committee members will need to develop and maintain their skills and knowledge, including an understanding of the committee's responsibilities and of the company's business, operations, and risks.

Job Title	Reports To
Inside Sales Executive	Sales Manager

Purpose:
- To generate qualified leads and book initial sales meetings and workshop attendance.
- To provide marketing, administrative, prospecting, and sales support including client relationship management, maintaining the CRM system, running the marketing activities, and maintaining the website.
- To enable the company to achieve its business development targets, sales targets, and overall business strategy.
- To work in partnership with colleagues to enable them to meet their objectives of incremental revenue growth and improved overall sales productivity and new account penetration.

Key Accountabilities

- Make outbound calls to cold and partially qualified records within the company's target market database. Call key decision makers from a broad range of industry sectors and deliver agreed results. Identify the key pains or issues the prospects are experiencing.
- Achieve the required goals for each designated campaign: attendance at a directors briefing, a face-to-face meeting, a telephone meeting, agreement to complete a questionnaire, etc.
- Establish account presence and build trust with key contacts within the target market.
- Develop and maintain the CRM system. Capture data and notes from the phone calls into the CRM system accurately, including dates for follow-up calls; manage email sending; add individual records or bulk uploads.
- Achieve KPIs for volume of activity, results achieved, quality of data, conversions, etc. Communicate results and developments to colleagues as required.
- Manage personal sales and prospecting administration.
- Work effectively as part of a team, directing co-sellers on a client account, especially in areas of learning.
- Take responsibility for following up with prospects, ensuring they complete any pre-attendance questionnaire and confirming attendance at workshops.
- Study prescribed CDs, videos, or reading; undertake these and other personal development activities in order to develop knowledge of effective sales techniques.
- Undertake other reasonable duties and project work as directed by the sales manager.

Financial Scope (limits/mandates, etc.)	People Responsibility (customers/staff, etc.)
No financial accountability.	No staff responsibility. Responsible for developing and maintaining relationships with prospects, clients, and colleagues.

Knowledge, Qualifications, and Experience:

- Proven successful track record in a target-driven outbound sales environment.
- Experience selling solutions in business-to-business markets.
- Experience selling to prospects at all levels.
- Ability to consistently implement sales techniques within own area of responsibility.
- Reasonable understanding of the broader sales methodology.

Expectations, Skills, and Behaviours:

- Enjoys working with customers and building relationships; strong interpersonal communication (spoken and written), and listening skills.
- A polite, professional, confident, persuasive, and authentic telephone manner; solid telesales skills and aptitude.
- Shows initiative and demonstrates the drive required to be successful.
- A positive attitude to work and strong customer-service orientation.
- Flexibility, adaptability, and quick thinking; the ability to quickly absorb information about clients' companies and range of solutions.
- Perseverance and the ability to respectfully challenge customers' answers.
- Well-organised and thorough, even under pressure.
- Enjoys working within a target-driven team environment.
- Understands and complies with the legislation relating to direct marketing.
- Self-motivated and happy to work independently; a positive attitude for work.
- An openness and enthusiasm for change and improvements to the business.
- The drive and determination to make things happen.
- Gets a kick out of making sales coupled with strong determination to make sales.
- A good team player, prepared to dive in when required.
- Proficient with email and Microsoft Office Suite, prior experience using a CRM system, and confident with computers.
- Good focus on the detail of presentation and quality of information.
- Skilled at multi-tasking and prioritising, particularly under tight deadlines.
- Excellent people skills for working with a range of colleagues and clients especially via phone and electronic media.
- A willingness to work long hours, often under pressure.
- Works well with others, demonstrates teamwork, seeks to understand and meet clients' needs and find solutions.
- Learns and implements consistently all areas of effective selling technique.

Scope and Complexity (including thinking challenge, innovation, managerial challenge, strategic impact):

- The work is fast-paced and intense, and this position has only a short amount of time to build rapport with customers and get results.
- Work is performed with minimal direction and supervision; assignments are well-described and delivery is reviewed upon completion for quality and meeting objectives within deadlines set.
- This position independently suggests approaches to solutions with some overview prior to implementation.
- This position contributes ideas of improvements to client projects proactively.

Leadership Challenge (including mentoring, role modeling, etc.):

Responsible for own work with possible coordination of client-facing activities.

KPIs/Key Deliverables:	
KPI Area Campaign coordination	KPIs
Quality	Number of meetings that turn into sales. Quality of meetings set up as judged by salesperson.
Productivity	Number of quality meetings booked. Number of dials per day. Number of minutes spent on the phone talking to prospects.
Organisation and structure	Accuracy of CRM notes. Timely follow up with prospects.

Chapter Summary

This chapter has been all about defining and templating. Key messages include:

- All your jobs need to be well defined. This is important when hiring but also when managing performance. People need to know what is expected of them if they are to excel.
- When hiring you need to specify the ideal candidate to provide a benchmark against which you can qualify and select candidates.
- Focus on hiring A-Players or Winners.
- Consider team fit but remember that this is not so much if the person will get on with everyone but more about the overall team make up and strengths and filling in gaps.
- High performance should not be confused with ambition or high potential (promote-ability), You want high performers in all your roles but will not be able to promote everyone (unless you are in a very rapid growth phase) so balancing this out when hiring is critical.
- Hiring inexperienced people can provide a great source of

talent but requires the right skills (spotting potential) and infrastructure (training, mentoring, etc.).

- When hiring Millennials, do not stereotype but take into account their particular needs both during the hiring process and once they join.
- Apply the SEARCH model (skills, experience, attitude, results, cognitive skills, habits or competencies).

CHAPTER 5

Prospect and Attract

iring, as we have outlined in earlier chapters, is a process. The better prepared you are, the more systematic you will be in executing that process and the better the results will be.

The search for talent (also known as prospecting) can be undertaken as a one-off exercise, as an annual campaign, or as a continuous process. There will of course be times when you need to treat this as a one-off exercise (for instance, you have a sudden requirement for a scarce skill or your organisation is moving into a new geography or specialty).This is to be expected, and indeed it might be where you can benefit from working with a recruitment agency (see Chapter 9). At other times a campaign approach might make sense; for instance, graduate recruitment is typically managed on a campaign basis due to the seasonality of the availability of new graduates and the infrastructure put in place by many academic institutions, such as career fairs and career services functions.

Even given these exceptions, the reality remains that the more you can take a continuous approach, the greater your chance of successfully attracting a wide range of top talent—not just that which is readily available at the point in time that you realise you need it.

This chapter looks closely at forecasting from the recruiter's point of view. Its assumption is that the more you can plan ahead for demand and the more sources and platforms you have for recruiting talent, the more choice and availability you will have when you need it.

Forecasting: An Overview

If you are to have any chance of being ahead of the game with recruitment, you need to be able to forecast demand. Forecasting in recruitment is similar to forecasting in business. You look at past data, you look for indicators of change in the future, and you place your best bet. A recruitment forecast needs to be dynamic and regularly updated, but equally it needs to be sufficiently robust to direct investment, time, and attention.

Past data includes the numbers and roles that you have recruited for in the past. It should also include information on staff turnover rates by roles (and locations where appropriate).

Forecasting is thinking ahead to what you will need in the future. Is your company growing, changing focus, entering new markets, expanding to new territories/geographies? You need to forecast out as far as you can. Use your business five-year plan to map out the organisation you will need in five years' time.

Once you have this information (past data and future

forecasts), you need to map it onto your current organisation architecture. This will allow you to see if your organisation structure will remain the same or if, in the medium to long term, it will differ significantly. In turn, this will give you an idea of the number and types of roles you will need in the future.

You now have the roles you believe you need in the future and the roles you have at present, with likely churn for those roles. If you are doing recruitment forecasting for a huge organisation, you will probably simply work off ratios—the percentage expecting to leave, the percentage you expect to promote internally, etc.

If you are looking at forecasting within a single function with one manager, then you can go into this in more detail. In these circumstances, it is helpful to have a clear forecast for each of your people. By this I mean, that for each individual, you undertake an annual planning exercise looking at where they are, where they are likely to progress, risk of them leaving, and criticality of their leaving. This is a slight digression from recruitment in its strictest sense but it does qualify under the broad definition of resourcing being more than just hiring new external talent but also about development of current talent and organisational design and development.

I recommend the following table to my clients.

Name	Performance (H/M/L)	Length of service (years)	Current role	Time in current role (years)	Likely next role	Time to next role (years)	Risk of leaving (H/M/L)	Impact of leaving (H/M/L)	Actions required to retain and grow
Jane	High	4	Salesperson	3	Sales Mgr.	1	L	H	Find ways to develop team management, e.g., project leadership, training, etc.
John	High	6	Salesperson	4	Same	n/a	M	H	Look at ways to keep motivated, perhaps move to new product or market.
Chris	Med.	3	Inside Sales	3	Outside Sales	2	H	M	Explore option to fast track to outside sales role.
Joe	Low	2	Inside Sales	1	Same	n/a	L	L	Improve or exit.
Rob	Low	2	Inside Sales	2	Same	n/a	M	L	Encourage exit.

Completing a table such as this will give you information on where you might be losing people (as well as actions for mitigation).

To be able to develop your requirements in the next one to five years, you need to have information on your overall business plan. This will give you an idea of sales volumes, which will enable you to develop the organisation you will need to meet those volumes and where you will have vacancies.

The next table illustrates what this might look like for a small, high-growth company.

	Current Year	Year 2	Year 3	Year 4	Year 5
Forecast Sales Volumes	xx	xx	xx	xx	xx
Sales Directors	0	1	1	1	1
Sales Managers	1	1	2	2	3
Sales Team Leaders	0	0	0	1	0
Salespeople	8	13	19	25	32
Sales Support	1	1	2	3	3
Inside Sales	0	5	5	6	7
Account Managers	1	1	2	2	3
Account Execs	0	1	1	2	2

The table following summarises recruitment requirements. In the table I have separated new staff (new recruits due to needing more staff for the role) and replacement for staff turnover (new recruits needed to replace those who leave or are promoted) to make it easier to follow the numbers. In both cases, new recruits are not needed if the need for new staff or replacements required due to staff turnover can be met by internal promotions or moves.

For example, take Year 4 and the sales manager role. In Year 4, the table is not anticipating increasing the number of sales managers but is expecting that natural turnover will mean that the company will lose one. So, it is 0 (new) + 1 (replacement).

Also in Year 4, the sales team leader has 0 for recruitment because the company believes that this role will be filled by one of its salespeople. You can see that there is an extra role under replacement, with 3 for staff turnover and 1 for the vacancy arising from the promotion.

	Current Year	Year 2	Year 3	Year 4	Year 5
Sales Directors	0	1	0	0	0
Sales Managers	0	0	1	0 + 1	0 (assumes promotion)
Sales Team Leaders	0	0	0	0 (assumes promotion)	0
Salespeople	0	0 + 2	1 + 2	4 + 4 (assumes 2 promoted from inside sales)	4 + 4
Sales Support	1	1	2	3	3
Inside Sales	0	5	0 + 2	0 + 4 (2 promoted)	3 + 2
Account Managers	1	0	1	0 (promotion to cover turnover)	1
Account Execs	0	1	0	2 (assumes 1 is promoted)	0

You now have a recruitment forecast and know for which positions you need to gear up. This knowledge will allow you to hire in line with seasonal availability of talent; for example, new graduates entering the marketplace even if you do not have an immediate vacancy. Hiring graduates when they first come onto the market generally gets you access to higher talent (a bit like a first-round draft pick in sports) or even a high-quality speculative application or referral you would otherwise not be confident of being able to fit into your company.

Finding: Efficient, Effective, and Creative Sourcing

To efficiently and effectively find the best recruits, you need to have a multifaceted, pipeline approach incorporating these elements:

- **Online recruitment.** Recruit online through a career portal and the effective use of social media and job boards. There are many benefits of having a career portal, somewhere that all prospective applicants can visit to learn about the company, its jobs, its people, and its vacancies and also to apply directly. This increases engagement with interested people and keeps them focused in one place where you can make core information available without cluttering up your business website. It also allows direct applications, which reduces the drop out between them learning about a role and applying. Direct inbound applications are the lowest-cost talent acquisitions, just as direct inbound sales have the lowest cost of sales. They are a good thing. Strong career portals keep the same branding but

I was at an international airport with multiple flight delays including my own and spotted a 16- or 17-year-old student on his last day of a one-week work experience. He was fielding a long queue of frustrated passengers, many of whom did not speak English, while the full-time staff appeared to have abandoned the desk. I was impressed. I gave him my business card with the promise of a job any time he wanted one.

have a separate URL (job.XCo.com, careers.XCo.com, and so on). They should have information on the company (who you are, what you stand for, ambitions and plans, performance, awards and recognition, and history) as well as general employment information (culture, leadership, rewards, diversity and inclusion, and learning and development). Include an overview of the jobs you have in the company as well as real employee stories. Add your social links. The portal needs to be authentic, use real employees and not actors, and never use stock photography.

- **Referrals and talent spotting.** Spot talent through systematic data capture from managers and staff. This is one of the most effective ways of finding and hiring talent. It needs to be incorporated into your company culture: "This is such a great place to work, I want to invite people in." You need to have a process for managing employee referrals. If you handle them well, you will get more; if not, they will dry up. We cover Millennials later (they love referring, if they love you). Talent spotting should be a way of life. When I go to a conference or event, I bring back the names of at least two or three people I met that I think would be a great addition to the company. When I am shopping and I spot the checkout person or bagger who is going the extra mile, I think, "Would that person do this for us?" This needs to be part of the culture but also part of the process.

- **Referral reward schemes.** I would be remiss if I did not include in this section the option of developing reward schemes that pay existing employees for bringing in new recruits. As it happens, I personally dislike this approach— I think that you should build an organisation culture that generates these referrals without paying a bounty on each head. However, I recognise that there will be some circumstances where this approach is appropriate. If introducing a candidate referral reward scheme, make sure you build in some minimum success criteria; e.g., the payment is only made after the new hire passes probation. You will also want to make sure that your employees are recommending the candidate based on personal experience, not just throwing names over the fence. Consider having the introducer mentor the new recruit for their first six months.

- **Talent pools.** Build relationships with and keep in touch with people who could fill vacancies as they arise. This includes people who have expressed an interest in working with you and the people that you have talent spotted. You need to develop ways to engage your talent pools, and they do not always need to be linked to hiring. Use them to beta test products, ask their opinions, and get them involved.

- **Alumni.** Keep in touch with people who have left since they may return and they will be networking with others; e.g., annual holiday or New Year's messages and updates. Get them involved as well. For example, seek their views and inputs on marketing campaigns, new products, and similar initiatives.

- **Talent mapping.** This is an effective way to track down particular skills and locate top talent and plays an important role in any recruitment strategy. You can do this yourself, or you can hire companies to do this for you. You can do this from two sides—either mapping all the talent in a company, or mapping a single talent type across a sector or geography (or potentially globally if you operate in the global arena). To illustrate the latter, let's say you are looking for top-performing salespeople regardless of sector but limited to a geography. You then map where they are using multiple information sources such as awards and recognition, LinkedIn, company websites, etc. For smaller companies, you can do this a bit more pragmatically—who are the salespeople you hate to come up against when pitching for new work, who are the people winning local business awards, and so on.

- **Events, conferences.** Take the opportunity to systematically scout for talent at all events and conferences. For example, if any staff members attend outside events, conferences, or courses, they should be tasked to report back on the talent they spotted. This information should be followed up on. At most companies, being funded to attend such events is a significant bonus (if this is not the case, I would encourage you to develop this approach). Part of earning their attendance fee should be providing you with a list of the three to five most qualified people they meet. This is easy to do and a great way to build a list of top external talent that can then be approached when you have vacancies.

- **Trade shows.** Look out for talent running the stands; this can be especially effective if you are recruiting salespeople. Who are the most effective salespeople in the booths? What makes them effective? Get their names and connect with them later. Do not try to recruit them at the event; it is not classy, and you might find people doing it to your talent.

- **University recruiting.** Build strategic relationships with one or two universities. Graduate recruiting, namely hiring cohorts of new graduates, takes some organisation. You are also in direct competition with all the other employers. It can sometimes be useful to find ways to engage with graduates before they graduate so that you can hook them without getting embroiled in a career fair. Building relationships with a small selection of colleges and universities is a good way of getting known. If you can offer work experience, training, etc., all the better.

- **Building relationships with schools** (pre-university, secondary schools, and high schools). Sponsor awards and competitions, run a work-experience scheme, allow for work shadowing, and give career talks. Not only does this kind of initiative raise your profile in your local community (which will help you attract candidates), but it also helps you identify specific kinds of talent and keep track of that talent. Years ago, I worked in research and development at a company that sponsored a multi-school science competition. One year I acted as the judge and was simply blown away by the talent of the students. Our R&D director gave a short keynote speech that ended with him announcing that if anyone on the competing teams ever wanted a job, they should contact him personally. He meant it! This is a great example of a strong recruiting and talent-spotting culture in action.

- **Speculative applications.** Managed effectively, these can be a useful source of candidates. You will get speculative applications, especially if you have a portal and your staff are networking and recommending you as an employer. Clearly not all will be suitable, but handling each with dignity and respect will enhance your brand. The on-target ones can be added to your talent pools if you don't happen to have a suitable job at that moment.

- **Special campaigns.** These include graduate recruitment, school leavers, customer service teams, and so on. Graduates are covered above, but think about other groups of people and where you can find them. Find a way to get in touch with them. How about leafletting at your local supermarket?

- **Sourcing creatively.** Think about the less obvious sources of people who will have the attributes you are looking for. This is particularly useful in roles where the time to effectiveness is not long and you can teach employees the knowledge and skills they need to be successful. For example, if you are looking for call centre staff, with people handling inbound enquiries rather than making outbound telesales calls, you might think about handing out flyers to supermarket checkout staff leaving at the end of a shift. If you can be flexible on hours or months of work, a great source of candidates would be parents of children at local schools who might be interested in working during school hours. You can usually advertise these sorts of opportunities on school noticeboards. Involve your employees; many of them will have children at the local schools and can help you to get your job opportunities known.

- **Strong strategic focus.** Short-term requirements need to balance with long-term strategic considerations. This is easy to write but harder to do, especially when sitting with one or more vacancies. The key is to work on hiring before it becomes a crisis.

- **Centralised recruitment budget.** This allows for economies of scale, optimising spending and assuring consistent messaging. You need to take a portfolio approach, placing some longer-term bets (alumni circles, strategic relationships with universities) and some shorter-term actions (using a recruitment agency). There will be some funding required (career portal, applicant tracking systems). This all needs to be balanced and monitored to ensure you are getting a decent Return on Investment (ROI).

- **Measurement culture.** Establish a measurement culture with clear metrics and continuous improvement. Measurement needs to be positioned as a way to learn and develop rather than punish. The metrics need to be tracked and then acted upon. Use qualitative data as well; talk to those who can give you valuable insights and suggestions for improvement, especially recent hires. Perhaps even let them implement the suggestions.
- **Recruitment partners.** Establish partnerships with one or two external recruitment partners. This is covered in more detail in Chapter 9.
- **Clear HR and line roles.** Ensuring that all involved know what they doing clearly makes sense. This is important in recruitment where tensions can arise between these two groups. The most common are: managers getting frustrated because they cannot take on a new recruitment agency; HR getting frustrated that the manager is taking too long in shortlisting or finding time to interview; managers annoyed that candidates are dropping out, and so on.
- **Company brand.** Clear, congruent employer brand with a compelling/competitive employment value proposition is needed. This is fundamentally important, not just in terms of hiring but also retaining top talent.
- **Talent management processes.** These need to be fully aligned with your business strategy and direction. Have a look at your processes. Are they all contributing to taking the business forward? Are they fit for your purpose? Processes need to deliver an output; it is the output that matters. A succession plan with lots of names that is diligently filled in is no use if when the time comes nobody on the list is deemed suitable.

Sourcing Is Critical

If you don't utilise sources that attract a high percentage of top performers, it is unlikely you will make a quality hire. After employment branding, effective sourcing is the most critical element of the finding and attracting process.

Measure the effectiveness of your sourcing channels to see which are working well and which need improving or are simply wasting time and money.

Pipeline Approach

Your goal as a recruiter must be to accumulate a steady stream of qualified applicants—what salespeople might refer to as a pipeline. To do this, you must start recruiting in advance of there being a vacancy. This strategy, called a pre-need approach, includes workforce planning, branding, continuous sourcing, and strategic recruitment.

Part of building a pre-need approach is good forecasting, as described above. This allows you to predict when you may need people and to recruit for the prediction.

It also helps to undertake an analysis of the jobs within the department or company and start to identify clear entry roles that can, with good candidates coupled with training and development, progress to these other roles. An example might be hiring to inside-sales roles and developing people to outside-sales roles. Not everyone will progress, but if you know where you are wanting people to go, you can recruit to this long-term requirement as well as the immediate job. Progression does not need to be limited to your own functional area. You can liaise with people in other parts of the organisation and offer a pipeline of talent to them. The benefit here is that you can hire people to entry roles with decent career prospects, which increases your ability to attract top talent.

Target Those Not Actively Looking

The best recruiting processes are designed to identify and successfully hire currently employed top performers. This means that the process needs the ability to identify individuals employed by your competitors or who work in other industries but whose skills are transferable that you consider to be top talent and would greatly enhance your organisation's performance. You also need, or need to develop, the capability to convince these employed individuals that they should join your organisation even when they may not be actively looking for a position.

Technology

The best processes rely heavily on technology and your online presence in all aspects of the recruiting process. Technology can improve screening, increase hiring speed, cut costs, and provide the firm with the capability of hiring globally.

An effective career portal offers a number of benefits:

- Provides a single source of applications for a job.
- Allows you to engage and interact with internal and external candidates.
- Offers multimedia information to prospective candidates—web, downloads, video, information, and advice.
- Tracks progress on a campaign or an individual application.
- Allows for measurements against key performance indicators, performance evaluations, and feedback.

Applicant Tracking Systems

Depending on how much recruitment you undertake, this can range from a spreadsheet to a highly sophisticated, fully integrated online system that talks to your HR system (or your CRM) and automates all your communication with applicants.

A spreadsheet will work fine if you hire a few people each year and one at a time. However, if you hire a lot of people, particularly if you are seeking to attract school leavers and graduates where you will be handling a high volume of candidates, having an application management or applicant tracking system will pay dividends. Not only will it save you time, but also the candidates' time as well. You will also increase your "curb appeal" with applicants who will have a swifter, easier interaction with you, which will enhance your employee value proposition. This will increase your access to top talent.

Whether or not you use a fully functioning system or a more manual one, you should invest time in creating standard letters for acknowledging applications, asking candidates to complete assessments, and invitations to interview. Once again, this will give you an additional edge when seeking to hire.

Attracting

This means both attracting the right candidates and being attractive to targeted candidates.

It's great when a steady stream of qualified candidates reaches out to you, but this does not happen overnight. It is the result of planning, time, and attention. If, as an organisation, you have significant ongoing hiring requirements in specific areas, it makes sense to invest in reaching a point where virtually all your recruitment for those positions is through inbound enquiries. Sales and customer service roles are often great examples in which significant benefits can be gained from achieving high levels of inbound enquiries and being able to hire directly for all of your roles. When coupled with some of the branding benefits of having a strong presence in the hiring marketplace, increasing your investment in generating direct, inbound hires can make a lot of sense.

Yet it's important to understand that inbound job enquiries are not always possible or desirable. Even if this is your business strategy for certain positions, you should be flexible enough to decide on occasion that a different approach is required—for example, when looking to hire a new skill set where you do not have a strong reputation in the hiring marketplace or when you need to attract people who are not looking to change jobs. If you limit your search for candidates to only those who are actively looking for work, you will end up reducing the size of your talent pool.

With all of that in mind, consider these suggestions on how to enhance your ability to attract inbound job enquiries:

- **Do your research.** Think about what will make you stand out in the hiring marketplace. The elements in Chapter 2 covering the 4Ps and your SWOT exercise will help with this. Engage with your people and ask them what they like and don't like about working with you. Check out the feedback you get on sites such as Glassdoor. Ensure that you carry out meaningful exit interviews with anyone who leaves your organisation voluntarily. Use this information in your online messaging. One of the processes I work through with leadership teams when working with them to improve recruitment within an organisation is to help them develop six to eight key themes—things that they stand for and believe in, their purpose beyond profit. They then use these themes consistently across their social footprint. It keeps the message focused and congruent.

- **Make it easy for potential candidates to learn about**

your company and your jobs. Having a compelling career portal on your website that is easy to find and fully aligned with your employee value proposition is critical. This needs to be supported by a strong LinkedIn company page and Facebook page. Ideally your social presence will focus on working in and joining your company. Include real people's stories and their experiences in both joining (being hired) and working for your organisation. Make sure the stories are true to life. If they come across as too "glossy," they won't feel authentic and may do you more harm than good.

- **Use the tools outlined in this chapter, ensuring you have a forecast for your hiring requirements.** Knowing what you are looking for will improve your chances of attracting it. Manage your pipeline, and properly track its candidates.

- **Perhaps most important of all, make sure you are geared up to deal with inbound job enquiries.** Ideally you should have an online, automated way of collecting and dealing with applications, especially speculative ones. Given that you are encouraging people to reach out to you, you need to be able to treat them well when they do. Simply saying, "Sorry, we do not have a vacancy; please try again later," is not going to cut it and will damage your brand and reputation as a recruiter. You need to instantly acknowledge the application, tell the candidate what is going to happen, and give them timescales (and stick to them). If they are applying speculatively, you need to be able to separate out the ones that might be suitable for a future role from the ones that are unlikely to fit your future needs and deal with them accordingly.

Pipeline Management

The concept of pipeline management in recruitment is similar to that in sales. The fuller your pipeline, the greater your choice. Being able to choose the strongest candidate from an already strong field is the pinnacle for which all recruiters strive.

Filling your pipeline is a continual activity, not a one-off, high-concentration activity you undertake when you have a vacancy. Keeping your pipeline alive also takes time and attention. You need to nurture your pipeline candidates. Typically pipeline in recruitment comprises the following groups of people:

- Alumni
- Prospective applicants
- On-hold applicants
- Active candidates (i.e., currently in the process)

Tracking the number of people in your pipeline is a sensible discipline for those roles where you know that you will need to be hiring people often. It will give you information on the likelihood of your being able to fill vacancies as they arise.

Alumni

Maintaining contact with your alumni, particularly ones you regret losing, is a very effective recruitment tool. It achieves three things:

1. It keeps the door open with that population of alumni you hope might rejoin your company at a future date. All big firms who are serious about talent attraction invest some time and attention in their alumni. It works just as effectively with small firms. Social platforms make it much easier these days as well.

2. It acts as a source of candidate referrals. Alumni who have some level of engagement with your firm after leaving are much more likely to recommend that friends, family, and colleagues looking for a new job consider your company. You can rely on spontaneous referrals, or you can seek to stimulate referrals by sharing vacancies with and seeking help from your alumni.

3. Alumni can also prove to be a rich source of business or sales referrals, of knowledge, and of sharing best practices.

Prospective Applicants

Building a pipeline of prospective applicants is another important pipeline-filling activity. This can be done in a direct or indirect

At one of my previous companies, we used to run a two-week summer school for university students between their second to last and final year. It was aimed to give insights into top-quality graduates and build a bit of collateral with them. It had mixed results.

However, on introducing a small change, we increased our ability to hire the best graduates year-on-year. This change was to offer the top performers a job, with a contract, at the end of the summer school. We did not force them to sign in advance, but we gave them full security of the offer. It was then held open until their graduation date. Many of them opted out of the usual university hiring fair activities and simply joined us. They effectively took themselves out of the recruitment market and were not available to our competitors.

way. An important metric is to measure the number of potential hires you have in your hiring pipeline.

Direct would be to make direct contact with people with the idea that at some point they might want to be candidates. This works particularly well if you target potential future recruits while they are still at school or university. Done well, it will also contribute to your local footprint and corporate social responsibility branding. If school-related activities are part of your strategic recruitment, you need to plan carefully which schools and which graduates you most want. You also need to have a well-designed journey for them to follow that increases engagement and ensures you are well-placed as a potential employer at the point they are looking. You can also design your interactions to give information on these potential candidates in advance so that when the time comes you can act swiftly.

Indirect is when you engage and build relationships with a wide network in anticipation that you will be recruiting in the future and will want to be able to reach out to this group. Here social and networking platforms are integral to your strategy. As with all prospecting, it is about a little and often. Making connections with people who fit your profile on LinkedIn is a long-term pipeline-building exercise (LinkedIn is also a short-term search source, of course).

On-Hold Applicants

The third group of pipeline candidates are those who have approached you, were not suitable for the job you had at the time, but nevertheless looked to be very high calibre. Here I am suggesting more than simply asking if you can store their CV. I am suggesting that you actively keep in touch with these individuals and nurture them so that when you do have a suitable job they will positively jump at it.

All of these pipeline-building activities are focused on building and engaging with talent pools. Exactly as with a sales pipeline, you need to keep in touch and keep them warm. Building talent pools means that you should build into your normal work routine time to meet with and interview potential top talent, openly explaining that while you don't have the perfect role for them today, you might in the future. Budgeting time and money for talent pools and pipeline management is critical if you are to derive value and improve your ability to recruit top talent.

Centralised Recruitment

Creating a business-level recruitment budget is an important foundation for building strategic recruitment capability. While the precise number of vacancies that might arise is hard to determine, your work on trend analysis and forecasting should give you a good enough idea to create a budget. At the strategic end, some investment is required for pipeline building and maintenance rather than just vacancy filling.

For smaller organisations, the debate about centralised vs. decentralised recruitment accountability and budgeting is moot, but in larger organisations it can be a topic of considerable debate. I am a believer in a central function and budget for the following reasons:

- **Cost savings.** Costs can be reduced or redirected to more strategic activities through leveraging resources, driving efficiency, and controlling spending.
- **Control.** Standardised policies and procedures lead to fewer errors and increased operational efficiency. Who would you prefer to perform your eye-laser surgery? Someone who does 50 every day, or someone who does one each week? Focused effort also reduces risk.

- **Change.** Change is easier and faster. Centralised recruitment facilitates the introduction of improvements and technology and helps to more smoothly integrate social and network changes.
- **Quality.** Quality of both the process and the output (i.e., the hires) is improved through greater experience, focus, and benchmarking.
- **Employment brand.** There are more opportunities to strengthen the employment brand, which increases attractiveness in the marketplace and access to top talent.
- **Innovation.** A high-performing dedicated team results in creating innovation—in terms of process improvement, selection approach, and candidate attraction.

As processes become embedded and part of the culture, a more hybrid approach can be adopted in which execution can be more localised but strategy, the employee value proposition, and engagement are retained centrally.

Partnering

As with all business activities, a decision needs to be made as to how much should be done in-house and how much through partners. This decision needs to be taken in light of many factors, including business model, company size and sector, cost/benefits, opportunities, competence, and so on.

In the recruitment space, you have a multitude of options around recruitment partnering, and there are a wide range of agencies from which to choose.

At one end, you can effectively outsource all your recruitment through recruitment process outsourcing (RPO). Typically, RPO solutions are sold on cost benefits, and in some areas this might be sufficient. A better approach is to view this as strategic partnering with your business model—one that focuses solely on core activities. Unless your company is vast and global, you will probably get better results from working with a smaller firm that can grow with you in a full partnership.

At the other end, you might use an agency to locate hard-to-find skills that you need only periodically, and it is therefore not cost effective to build engagement and a pipeline of your own. In this role, agencies become a source of candidates and are part of your candidate-attraction channel.

I believe that recruitment agencies, at least the good ones, have a role to play in any recruitment strategy. The extent to which you seek to engage with them can vary, but what should stay unchanged is the approach that you take with agencies. If you approach the use of agencies as a short-term tactical solution, you will get exactly that. The experience and results will not be great. If you build a partnership with external agencies into your recruitment model and manage it well, you can increase your ability to find, attract, and hire that elusive top talent. (See Chapter 9 for more about working with recruitment agencies.)

Chapter Summary

This chapter has covered prospecting, attracting, and ensuring a strong candidate pipeline. Some key messages include:

- The stronger your candidate pipeline, the more choices you have—which in turn means the better your chances of hiring top talent.
- Forecasting is a critical component of successful hiring. It allows you to plan ahead with hiring and promoting, giving

you access to a greater talent pool and the ability to hire in advance and develop people for when you need them.

- To efficiently and effectively find the best recruits, you need to have a multifaceted pipeline approach to recruitment, including:

  - Online recruitment
  - Referrals and talent spotting
  - Talent pools
  - Alumni
  - Talent mapping
  - Events, conferences, and trade shows
  - University and school recruiting
  - Speculative applications
  - Special campaigns
  - Creative alternatives to traditional sources of candidates
  - Recruitment partners

- You should think creatively about sources of candidates, particularly if tried and tested sources are drying up or not giving you the quality of hire you need.
- Consider how you can make it easy for applicants to apply directly to your roles.
- Underpin your recruitment efforts with appropriate technology.

CHAPTER 6

Qualify and Select

A t its simplest, the qualifying and selecting step is a series of decisions as to whether or not the candidate should move to the next step in the process. Each element of the process therefore needs to fulfil this goal. In determining progression, you are simply looking at the match between the data you collected at that step and the requirements of the role. If the match is strong enough, the candidate should progress to the next qualifying step.

Strong selection competence requires the following:

- Strong selection methodology.
- Well-trained line managers and recruiters.
- The use of psychometric tools.
- The use of behavioural interviewing.
- Well-facilitated selection processes.

- Fact-based decision-making competencies.
- Timely decisions.

Inventorying

All recruitment carries risk. The inventorying step is the process whereby you build up an inventory of information on your applicants in order to minimise the risk. Your sources of information will include:

- Candidate's CV or resume.
- Candidate covering letter (these are less used these days but if supplied will provide additional information).
- Any additional information you ask candidates to send you as part of your application; e.g., examples of past work, designs, code, current sales plan, etc.
- Results of assessment tests that you have the candidate undertake.
- Assessment activities—role-plays, inbox exercises, analytical exercises.
- References.
- Core data.
- Telephone interview.
- Role performance evaluation.
- Work experience.
- Interviewing.

CV

Clearly the first information source you have on a candidate is the CV and potentially cover letter. If you specify in the application process what information you wish to see in the cover letter, you can also collect additional information. It might be necessary to make it very clear to applicants that you require this information so that if they do not provide it you can screen them out. If you do not make this explicit, you can find yourself in a situation where applicants don't provide the required information but you don't feel confident enough to use this fact to screen people out.

Assessment Tests

Testing can also provide a wealth of information. It is important to know why you are using a particular psychometric instrument and what you are looking for with it. For example, using a personality measure that gives you insights into leadership would be appropriate for hiring at the executive level.

Tests fall into five broad areas.

- **Behavioural and competency measures.** These measure individual behaviours and competencies—the candidates' predisposition to behave in ways associated with successful performance.

- **Aptitude or capability assessments.** Assessing capability or aptitude can be very difficult in a traditional interview setting but is a clear differentiator of performance. These tests reliably indicate the candidate's potential to develop required skills. They can also be particularly useful when candidates have limited or no prior work experience. The tests can measure a range of different areas including but not limited to: verbal and numerical reasoning, abstract or conceptual thinking, decision analysis, memory and attention, fault identification, and judgment.

- **Skills tests.** These test specific skills of an individual such as their ability to use Excel, Word, and other systems, as well as manual dexterity or spatial relations.

- **Values, motivation, and interests inventories.** These give insights into values and motivation. They can be useful in recruitment when they measure the motivation resonance or dissonance between individuals and organisations. An individual's resilience can also be evaluated.
- **Personality questionnaires.** These give you insights and let you speedily get to the heart of an individual's motivation, loyalty/integrity, emotional intelligence, decision-making approach, leadership style, communication and team working preferences, and a range of other factors that are important to work success. There are a number of these in the marketplace, and, used correctly, they can add information to your inventory of an applicant. They can assist recruitment and give the recruiter a way to explore a candidate in more depth during an interview.

When hiring, using a behavioural or competency assessment alongside a suitable skills or aptitude test (where required for the role) is one of the best ways to set yourself up for success. Personally, I would never recruit anyone without assessments. If given early in the process, provided it is a well-developed, properly accredited psychometric instrument, you can use it to short-list and save a huge amount of time. You also save angst since you screen out unsuitable candidates before you become emotionally invested in them and try to ignore the results. If you are going to use assessments, you need to take note of the results.

Another benefit of using assessments early in the process is that all the good ones will flag areas to explore during the interview, which can help you at this stage.

Using assessments to screen candidates means that you can cost-effectively screen very large numbers of people and evaluate

Once, after a long and tiring search for a salesperson, I found someone who did well at the interview, made a great mock cold call, but exhibited a few significant concerning aspects in a behavioural/competency assessment test. I decided that I would ignore the assessment test. Remember earlier I said that I could count my hiring failures on one hand? This was my fifth. I had become emotionally invested and made a bad decision.

them based on competency rather than CV. Most providers will sell you a multi-use license based on the number of hires you make rather than the number of assessments taken. This gives you access to people that your competitors might overlook, which gives you a competitive advantage in the search for talent.

Assessment centres provide even more evidence to add to the inventories of your applicants. These are typically one- or two-day events comprising a series of psychometric tests with other structured activities ranging from group discussions, role-play exercises, analytical exercises and report writing, presentations, and in-tray prioritising exercises. Once again, these activities need to be designed to achieve the desired outcome. Once you know what skills and competencies you are looking for, you can design a programme that gives you the ability to assess candidates against these.

References

References are another inventory tool if you carry it out as a phone call rather than simply sending over a form. You should get the candidates' permission to make these calls. Speak to at least two of their direct managers—their most recent included, if possible. In terms of timing, there will be situations when there is nobody the applicant will be comfortable having you speak with prior to an offer (for example, if they have only worked for one company and have not yet told them they are job hunting). If references cannot be checked prior to making an offer, the offer should be made conditional upon satisfactory references.

When making reference calls, you need to promise and deliver total confidentiality. Ask lots of open-ended questions, i.e., "Is there anything else I should know?" Let the referrer give you positives to build comfort before you ask for negatives. Take notes and check for understanding. Below is a telephone reference checklist.

Notes of Reference Conversation		
Candidate name		
Interviewer/date		
Job/period of employment with referee		
Name of referee		
Key Question Areas		
Working relationship		What was your relationship with the candidate? Were you the direct manager? For how long?
Confirmation of the job they did		Tell me about the job the candidate did—job title, main accountabilities?
Working style		Tell me a bit about the candidate's working style?
Ability to work under pressure		What sort of pressure did the candidate work under? How did the candidate cope with pressure? Can you give me an example?

Relationship building		How was the candidate at building relationships—prospects, clients, colleagues?
Management style		Did the candidate have any management responsibilities? How would you describe the candidate's management style?
Strengths		What do you see as the candidate's main strengths?
Limitations		What do you see as the candidate's main limitations?
Reason for leaving		Why do you believe the candidate left your company? What if anything did you do to keep the candidate there?
Perfect job		What would you consider the perfect job for the candidate? What would it include? What would it exclude?
Recommendation for hiring		Would you hire this candidate again? Why or why not?
Further information		Anything else you think I should know?

Social Media Data

It is good practice to have a look at an applicant's social media footprint. This gives you insights that, if treated appropriately, can add to your inventory of the candidate. LinkedIn and Facebook are two obvious places to check out your candidates, along with Twitter (if applicable). You need to treat the information on the more purely social sites sensibly (rather than LinkedIn, which is more business linked). You cannot judge this as information you collect at an interview. It should be used to paint a picture of candidates, rather than to judge them.

Core Data

Objective data is the final inventory element. This will be to check business cards (gives job title), pay slips, and bonus/commission plans. This allows you to validate the information provided to you by the candidate. Remember the statistics of people "embellishing" their CVs are extraordinarily high: anything from 1 in 5 to 50% depending on which survey you read.

When hiring executives, information on their bonus and share plans is important in addition to establishing what they were paid. You are looking for high performance as evidenced by their reward and therefore need to know the plan design so that you can evaluate the payments as high or low.

For sales roles, collecting information on commission is an important indicator of their success. Once again, this information needs to be evaluated in the context of their commission scheme.

Some Thoughts on Screening

Generally, all these above inventory tools are used at different points in recruitment as part of the screening process. Screening is the process by which you reduce the number of applicants to a more manageable number. Effective and consistent screening should be done against criteria established in light of the requirements of the role.

You will screen at more than one level and deploy different inventory elements in the screening.

Typically, there are two potential starting points. One is to

An assistant enters her manager's office with a two-foot stack of papers, plonks them on the desk, and says, "Here are all the applicant CVs for your vacancy. Good luck." As she is leaving, the manager calls her back and hands her the top half of the stack. "Send this lot a turn-down," the manager says. Somewhat indignantly the assistant remarks, "That's not right. You can't just turn them down without looking at their CVs." The manager responds, "Sure, I can. They're unlucky, and who wants to hire an unlucky salesperson?"

This is, of course, one way to screen applications—but perhaps not the one advocated by this book.

screen on CVs (the more common approach). This is a manual process and can be time consuming in situations where you might get a very large number of applicants. Also if you are looking to hire school or university graduates with little to no job experience, their CVs will not provide all that much information.

An alternative is to screen first using one or more psychometric questionnaires. This way you can set a minimum performance bar and only look at CVs of those above the bar. Clearly if you are doing this, you need to use a validated questionnaire that is approved by the publisher for recruitment. There is some cost associated with this, so you should look at the cost/benefits of the time saved. In many situations, the case will be made that it would be beneficial to do an initial screen of all candidates using one psychometric questionnaire (usually behavioural/competency). Take care to use a correctly developed questionnaire that has been developed for recruitment screening purposes and is backed by data demonstrating the performance bars are appropriate and do not illegally discriminate. You might add additional psychometrics later on as well for the candidates who have made it through the first few stages to investigate other aspects.

Designing Your Qualifying and Selection Step

You need to design your assessment process taking into account the role that you are hiring for as well as the content (number of roles, frequency of this type of hire, and so on). As you go through this process, you are screening candidates, taking some out of the funnel and moving some forward past a particular screening gateway. The number and types of gates you have, as well as the order in which they are applied, will depend on the role for which you are hiring.

To illustrate, I have provided a few different assessment designs for different roles.

Senior Executive

The challenge with hiring senior executives is that you most likely do not have a great deal of experience hiring them so have not developed that much of an internal benchmark. Additionally, you will not have a lot of people to help with the interviewing since they are going to be the most senior or one of the most senior people in your company. It can, therefore, be a useful investment to use an external company to undertake the initial evaluation process for you. Whether done externally or by yourself, the initial evaluation process should include CV screen, psychometrics, interviews, competency assessment, detailed referencing, and track record evaluation.

Do not be intimidated by their seniority and feel that you cannot ask them to undertake psychometrics. A well-designed battery of tests can provide a great deal of information quickly and effectively, and this applies equally to senior roles.

Establishing and evaluating the track record of a senior executive is a crucial part of your selection process. This can be done in part through analysis of their roles and their results (past company share price, business results, etc.). Look carefully also at their career progression. Have they moved steadily upwards taking on bigger challenges and more complex companies, or have they appeared to plateau or been moved to the sidelines (sometimes these can be called "special project" roles)?

The interview needs to be conducted as a two-way discussion. You need to be deciding on fit as much as competence at this point.

Here is a suggested assessment screening flow:

- **Step 1:** Initial evaluation
- **Step 2:** Interview
- **Step 3:** Board presentation
- **Step 4:** Further interview

Inside Sales or Customer Service Role (Phone Based)

These are roles that are conducted purely on the phone. You therefore need to think about your selection process a bit differently. It's a bit like *The Voice*, where initially the acts are decided on voice alone. Phone competence is what will matter here, not the visual impact or body language of the candidate. Retention is also critical to these roles, which traditionally have very high turnover rates. It is therefore important that your successful candidate understands and is going to be comfortable in the role.

For this role, your initial interactions should be phone based. You will also want to build an experience element into the process as well. The work experience activity will involve the candidate attending work for the day and sitting alongside one of your experienced operators. They should be encouraged to ask questions but also to make notes of questions, observations, etc. Toward the end of the day you can then talk with them about their day, asking for observations, concerns, etc. Then conduct a role performance activity where they are asked to role-play a couple of scenarios that will have come up during the day. This can be rounded off with a bit of an interview and a decision. Ideally you should be able to make an offer (subject to references) on the day.

Here is a suggested assessment screening flow:

- **Step 1:** Psychometrics
- **Step 2:** Telephone interview
- **Step 3:** Telephone based role performance activity
- **Step 4:** Work experience activity
- **Step 5:** Debrief
- **Step 6:** Role performance activity (you might role-play this at the workplace on the phone)
- **Step 7:** Interview

Salesperson (Inexperienced Candidates)

The challenge here is the potentially high number of candidates and a shortage of work-related information due to the fact that they have not worked before. Thus, your assessment screening process should focus on early screening of the candidates. Using an assessment test is a good way to manage these particular challenges.

A recommended assessment screening flow would be:

- **Step 1:** Online psychometric questionnaire with a clear performance bar
- **Step 2:** CV review and screen
- **Step 3:** Telephone screen/interview
- **Step 4:** Face-to-face interview—technical and behavioural, plus potentially one of the following:
  - Role performance evaluation
  - Assessment centre

Salesperson (Experienced Candidates)

Here you have more information but are still likely to be inundated with a large number of candidates. If this is the case, adopting the same approach as for inexperienced candidates would make sense. However, in addition you need to include at the face-to-face interview stage the request for the candidate to bring with them a copy of their current 90-day plan or ask them to develop a plan for their first 90 days in the role, should they be given it. It is important to get a sense of their prospecting behaviour and attitude, and this is an excellent way of doing so. While asking them to develop a 90-day plan for the role is a bit theoretical, it will give you an idea of the behaviour and attitude and will also give you something to judge them against should they get the role. An early red flag would be if by Day 3, they have not followed it.

Sales Manager

This is a role where it would make sense to start with a CV screen. Looking at previous roles and management experience is relevant.

- **Step 1:** CV review
- **Step 2:** Telephone interview

- **Step 3:** Face-to-face interview (behavioural) plus potentially one of the following:
  - Role performance evaluation
  - Assessment centre

Of critical importance to the success of this role is the sales manager's ability to manage the accountability and behaviour of their team. Your behavioural questioning should explore this aspect in detail. In terms of role performance evaluation, you should consider a couple of exercises: giving them data on a territory and asking for an analysis, or giving them data on a sales team (sales over the previous 12 months plus a short description of each individual's experience, skills, strengths, and weaknesses) and asking them to give a report back on the team as if they were doing a quarterly team report to the sales director. These sorts of exercises can be purchased (many need to be administered by a qualified person) or designed in-house. What you come up with does not need to be complex. Think about some of the challenges they will face or activities they will be responsible for, and work out a simple exercise. Get your existing managers to try it out as a road test, incorporate their feedback, and you will be ready to go.

Think carefully about job design when it comes to hiring a sales manager. Designing a role where your new, externally hired sales manager has a "player manager role" (i.e., they are both selling and managing) is highly risky. They will need to sell a product or service that they are not familiar with and will be watched carefully by the rest of the sales team. If this is your longer term goal, at the beginning you should position them as managing only (while ensuring that they know they will be doing both). They can, of course, jump in to help with a sale when one of their team is struggling and also set the tone by doing sales calls with the team.

CV Screening

Adopt a systematic approach of screening each CV and cover letter against the requirements of the role. These criteria should be set in advance and applied uniformly across all CVs. This saves a great deal of time because you can quickly scan the CVs looking for the required element, which is the fastest approach. It also improves effectiveness—you don't get caught up emotionally in the CV and cover letter and start making false selections, positive or negative.

It is important to stay objective through the screening process. Most people have certain prejudices, and everyone needs to take care that they do not impact screening. Being biased not only could mean that you do not hire the best candidate for the job but also that you pick someone unsuitable. Any strict criteria may well screen out a hidden gem, but statistically the time and effort that you save through this process will pay dividends. If any CVs look particularly strong but do not match the criteria you are screening against, you can always put them to one side and consider them for any other vacancies you might have. They can go into the talent bank you should be developing.

Your first screening (CVs against agreed screening criteria) will give you a long list. If it is too long you might need to review the CVs for a second time. However, the more experienced you become, the easier it will be to get through this process in one go.

Some additional things to watch for with sales CV screening:

- **Typos and poor grammar.** This is an interesting issue. Is this indicative of poor attention to detail, lack of cognitive skills or education, or simply a symptom of today's e-technology where people rarely write and rely on auto-correct on their smartphones to do the work for them? The relevance will depend on your role. If your candidate is for a customer/accounts role, you might need them to have top written communication skills—unless they are phone based only, in which case written skills are not relevant. Failing to have the CV checked is a somewhat rookie error. On the other hand, they might have awful English grammar but their mother proofread it for them and made it flawless. If written English is critical to the role, test them via a role performance evaluation. However, even if I let mistakes through the CV screen, I might ask candidates about it in the interview.

- **List of tasks but nothing on outcomes.** This would be something to explore at the telephone interview since it could just be poor CV writing.
- **Reference to sales quotas/targets but nothing very concrete.** This is something to check out more. Those of us who are trained in effective interview techniques will know to dig under the skin of wishy-washy words.
- **Superlatives.** Does the CV say "top salesperson," "skilled at...," "secured large..."? These make one ask: What is top? What do they consider skilled? What is large?
- **No direct prospecting experience.** If there is no direct evidence of successful prospecting, this is a red flag. They may have been given all their leads, which is fine unless you want them to prospect their own.

Telephone Screening

The purpose of the telephone screen is to judge if the candidate should be invited to a face-to-face interview. Given that you could be telephone screening a good number of candidates for your vacancy, you need to keep these very concise and ensure you derive the information you need to make the decision to move forward. For most roles you will be as interested in their phone manner and their ability to articulate their thoughts in a structured and coherent way as their answers to your questions.

You need to have a clear script and plan. You can find a template in the resource section.

- Open the call with a clear agenda. Confirm the purpose of the call, the duration (15 minutes maximum), your role, and their role. Make the applicant feel at ease and create the right environment for an effective screening call. (2–3 minutes)

- Candidate experience: Ask applicants to describe in no more than 2 minutes their professional career. Check any gaps or questions you have from their CV if these are material to the decision to invite them to a face-to-face interview. If they are not, leave this to the face-to-face interview since it will simply waste time and prolong the call. (5 minutes)

- Specific requirements: Ask direct questions to validate key competencies. My preference is to keep these quite broad. For example: "Tell me about something that you have done that you found personally challenging." "Tell me about a time you had to influence or persuade someone to do something they did not want to do." (5 minutes)

- Next steps: Discuss the next steps with the candidate. (2–3 minutes)

The following telephone interview form provides a useful prompt for telephone interviews.

Telephone Interview Checklist
• Make sure it is convenient for the individual to talk. • Take notes, as you will need to refer to these if you invite the individual for an interview. • The questions do not need to be as challenging as they would be for a face-to-face interview. • Remember this conversation may be the only impression the individual receives of your company so make sure it is a good one.

Candidate Name:	Role:
Interviewed by:	Date:

1. Introduction
Introduce self
Is it convenient to talk now? (You may have pre-arranged the telephone interview either yourself or through HR.)
This telephone interview will probably last 15 minutes. Is this convenient?
• The reason for a telephone interview is that we have received a number of applicants for this role and identified those with the strongest experience. • We therefore wish to talk to you to gain further information from you, and share further information about the role. • Based on this discussion, we may invite you in for the next stage of selection.

2. Opening questions (purpose is to put the individual at ease): • Can you tell me about your current role? • Can you briefly talk me through your CV? • Why are you interested in this role?	

3. Provide a brief description of your company and the role.
4. I have some questions I would like to ask in order to understand your technical knowledge.

Technical Question	Response

5. I have some questions that will help me understand your work style and behaviours.

Behavioural Question	Response
What have you done in your current role that you consider to be innovative?	
What contribution do you make to business performance in your current job?	
Add question	
Add question	
Add question	

6. Confirmation of details	
Salary expectations:	
Notice period:	

7. Next steps
We will be in touch within the next week to let you know next steps. —or— I am interested in taking your application further. Are you? ... Great. The next step will be to set up a phone demonstration. This will involve you making a call to [me/my colleague _____] within a two-hour window and persuading us to do something. —or— I am interested in pursuing your application further. Are you? ... Great. The next step will be to set up a face-to-face interview. Would you let me know your availability?

For completion after the interview:	
Recommended for interview:	Yes/no and why:
Phone demonstration date: Interview date:	
Points to explore further at next interview:	

Role Performance Evaluation

Looking at the role performance evaluation a bit further, when hiring salespeople one of the critical areas you will need to evaluate is telephone skills. For many, this will include cold sales calling. Given this, you should always include in your selection process a telephone evaluation. I advise that this be done after the telephone screening interview and before the face-to-face interview. This way you can confirm the details with the candidate on the phone call. Clearly, this should only be given to those who have passed your phone screen.

To illustrate this, here are some example instructions to applicants.

> Between the hours of 5 and 7 P.M. on Tuesday, February 12, you should make a call to this number [provide number]. If there is no reply or the phone is busy, you may leave a message, but if the call is not returned, you should phone back. It is your responsibility to get through. Start the call as if it were real; do not start by saying, "Hi, this is my cold call test."
>
> The purpose of your call is to persuade the person who answers the phone to do one of these four things:
>
> - Attend a free business workshop on a topic of your choice.
> - Allow you to run a charity stall on the person's work premises one lunch time.
> - Come and speak at a charity event that you are holding.
> - Buy a product or service (that you are familiar selling).

As the receiver of their calls, you need to adapt to the scenarios they select and challenge them but not make it impossible (e.g., be a bit reluctant, but don't shout, "Never!"). You are looking for how they conduct themselves, their resilience, their questioning and listening, how pushy or salesy they are, and how influential. For those readers who are trained in effective sales techniques, remember they won't be at this point.

Some positive indicators from the call include:

- Checks if this is a good time/bad time to speak.
- Asks questions and listens to the answers.
- Adjusts according to what you say.
- Perseveres and pushes past your initial reluctance.
- Adjusts their pace and volume to yours.

Some negative indicators would include:

- Lots of pitching of features and benefits.
- For charity ones—implies you are not a good person if you don't support.
- Talks a lot.

A variation to this is to provide the candidates with information about your product/service, and get them to call you (same rules as above on them initiating within a window of time, etc.) and try to book a meeting or sell it to you (depending on the product/service). I personally do not favour this approach because I think candidates can get too caught up in the product or service and this detracts from your ability to evaluate their potential as a salesperson.

Role performance evaluation may also include tests or exercises, such as an inbox exercise where a candidate is asked to read, evaluate, and respond to a number of customer emails ranging from asking for information to making a complaint. This tests their judgment and ability to prioritise, as well as their written skills and accuracy.

For sales and account managers, territory planning is a critical skill. Giving them information (this can be real company data or specially developed for the exercise) and asking them to develop a plan is a good way of testing their actual ability in this area. If you give them real data, use past data that is in the public domain or no longer commercially sensitive. You do not wish to give them proprietary information at this point since they might not join you and might use that information in their current company or the company that hires them. A great illustration of this, as mentioned earlier, is a recruitment agency client of mine who put a candidate forward for a sales director role who was working for a competitor. Despite his warning the company to not share confidential information with the candidate at this stage since he was not 100% sure that the candidate was serious about a job move and worried that he might have just been doing some competitor research, they did so and were somewhat dismayed when, on being offered the role, he turned it down and stayed with their competitor.

For executives, a role performance exercise would be to ask the executive to read the latest annual report (or accounts) and to give a short presentation to the board. You could also ask them to produce a business plan and present this. This will test both their commercial understanding and their presentation and communication skills (both being critical to this role).

Work Experience

For some roles, building in a day or few days of work experience can be a useful part of the selection process. This approach is frequently used in the creative sector where people are invited in for up to a week to work on the team. This provides a real opportunity to confirm skills as well as fit.

This approach also works well with inside sales roles in which it is important to ensure that the applicant fully understands the nature of the role to help mitigate the risk of high turnover.

Care needs to be taken to protect your commercial information and reputation when arranging work experience as part of your hiring process. Using a simple non-disclosure agreement is also good practice.

Once again, this should form part of a well-thought-through process in which both the candidate and you will gain a clear view of the work experience. You should pay them for their time, and you need to ensure that the experience is realistic to working with you as well as attracting them to the job and the company.

Interviewing

Interviewing is about collecting information on candidates to see if they are a match for the job requirements. A bit like selling, you should invest at least as much time in planning and preparing as you will in conducting the interview. This is critical, yet, alas, much like selling, often people invest large amounts of time and money securing candidates to interview and all too often wander into the interview after only re-reading the CV.

The problem with this is two-fold. First, you will not be able to find out as much information as you would have if you had been prepared. You will waste time. This means you will be guessing and making assumptions at the decision step, which is risky. Second, you will not impress the candidate. Believe me, candidates can tell if you are prepared or not. They are making judgments about you as a manager and employer. If you make a poor impression at this point, you will struggle to attract top talent who have choices and frequently exercise that choice. Both of these reasons also under-pin the need to have a proper environment for the interview, without disruption or interruption.

Despite a yearning to have been recruiting when it was the rage to do outrageous interviews (sitting behind a newspaper while the

bin is on fire; handing a freshly arrived candidate a pencil shout-
ing, "Sell it to me!"), I firmly believe that if you want to be able to
accurately evaluate candidates you need them to be comfortable
enough to open up with you. This means getting a bit into their
rhythm and building an element of rapport. You can test them,
naturally, but get them settled in first. You do not want to lose
top talent to your competitor just because they interview better
than you and discover talent when you miss it. The interview
should therefore not be an adversarial encounter. Putting pressure
on people makes them clam up, not open up. One of the reasons
for face-to-face interviews is to expose hidden issues. This will not
happen if candidates feel under pressure and view you as an enemy
combatant. The more comfortable they are with you, the more
they will reveal their true thoughts and feelings and the better
your ability to make a high-quality hiring decision.

Also, people's level of chattiness and bounce during an interview
is not necessarily indicative of the real them. Many people will be
nervous at interviews, whereas they might be quite self-confident
in their work. Nerves can make some people overly chatty and
others somewhat quiet. I have experienced both. A candidate who
was pretty over-the-top at the interview (indeed so much so that
I needed to intervene to ensure we hired her) was incredibly quiet
and reserved when she started working. I've also met candidates
who were quiet and controlled interviewees who then turned out
to be chatty and slightly out of control in the work environment. If
you are not sure they will fit in, simply describe the work environment (a bit boisterous, very quiet) and let them decide. Better still,
introduce them to some of their future colleagues.

There are two types of face-to-face interviews you should
design into your recruitment campaign: technical interviewing
and behavioural interviewing.

The technical or achievement interview aims to find out what candidates know and what they have done. It should explore their experience in different types of sales, what techniques they know, and when they use them. This interview is also used to check through candidates' CVs where there are gaps or questions (e.g., why they changed jobs especially when the move does not look consistent with their career progress).

Behavioural interviewing is finding out what behaviours the candidate typically exhibits, having first established your idea of what behaviours are linked to success in your role.

The rationale that underpins behavioural interviewing is that past behaviour is the best, if not the only, predictor of future behaviour. This style of questioning gathers data on what interviewees actually do in a situation rather than what they think they might do in the future or what they think they did. It uncovers interpersonal as well as technical skills and provides specific data to allow quality decisions to be made.

You are looking to capture and write down for later analysis specific statements describing what, in past situations, the candidate personally said, thought, did, and felt. Standard probing questions to use in this technique:

- "What did you do?"
- "What did you say?"
- "What were you thinking?"
- "What did you do next?"
- "How did you feel?"

Keep the job candidate away from current reflections on past performance or current opinions and attitudes. The types of question to use are open-ended ("Tell me about..."), probing ("So what you were thinking was..."), summarising ("Having done xyz, what happened next?"), and closed when appropriate ("Did it work?"). You should avoid questions that are leading ("Would it be fair to say that...?"), hypothetical ("Imagine you are leading a project that..."), or multiple choice ("Did you manage to xyz, or was it all abc?")

When using a behavioural technique, always interview in pairs and agree how the pair of interviewers will work together.

- Who will ask questions/take notes? (You can take turns if you like.)
- Agree who will do the introduction and close the interview.

In order to decide on your behavioural questions, use the job accountabilities or competencies to prioritise the behavioural qualities that will lead to superior performance in the role. Limit yourself to six (eight at the most) key areas. Ensure that you have two questions identified for each area. You may not need to use both, but it is essential to have a backup in case the first one does not give you much data. Your job is to get the information out of the candidate. Failure to get data is not a poor performance; it is a neutral performance. That is, you cannot judge them on it because that could well be as much the interviewers' fault as the candidate's. Evidence of poor performance is gathered when the candidate describes actions and thoughts that are a clear indication of the absence of the desired behaviour or adoption of a negative behaviour. These are negative indicators. Positive indicators are evidence of those behaviours aligned to superior performance.

The Interview Funnel

You may be familiar with the Sandler Pain Funnel® and with how powerful a tool it can be for salespeople. This is a series of questions that sequentially brings the prospect closer to sharing their true agenda or pain.

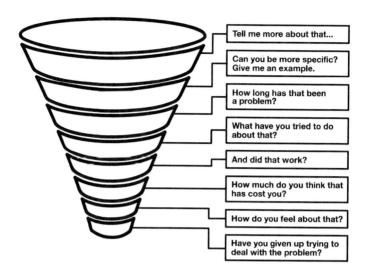

You can apply a similar approach to the interview. Start by opening things up and then keep narrowing them down.

Interview Funnel

Ask a broad open question.

Listen actively.

Pick up on a point that is relevant to the job/person and ask for more information.

Listen actively.

Ask probing questions to check detailed facts.

Listen actively.

Use reflective or probing questions to reveal motivations and feelings.

Listen actively.

Summarise and ask for confirmation or correction.

Here is an example to illustrate the difference between a weak candidate and a strong one. Weaker candidates tend to use wishy-washy language and be a bit more vague, forcing interviewers to ask additional questions to clarify, as the example shows.

Interviewer: Tell me about a time when you were asked by your manager to do something that you did not agree with. *[Broad, open-ended question.]*

Candidate: At the time there was an interest in selling into a new foreign geography, and my sales director wanted me to complete a number of tender documents. I did not really feel that this was a good approach.

Interviewer: When you say that you did not feel that this was a good approach, tell me what you mean. *[Picked up on candidate not feeling this was a good approach, and followed up.]*

Candidate: I felt that we didn't have much of a chance of success and it was going to take a lot of time and effort.

Interviewer: *[Probing questions on two issues to follow up: time/effort and chance of success.]* To give me an idea of what you mean by a lot of time and effort, tell me a bit more about your process. How many tenders were you doing each week or month and how long did you take to complete each one?

Candidate: We were doing one a week and initially it took me about three days to complete each one.

Interviewer: *[Picking up on the word "initially."]* You said that it was initially three days. How much faster did it get and how did this come about?

Strong Candidate: Well, I decided that if I was going to have to do a lot of tenders I needed a system to make things more efficient. I therefore put together all the information in a set of standard templates that I could cut and paste into and modify as necessary, rather than writing them all from scratch. I created three different core documents to cover the three sizes of projects that we were bidding for. This meant that each tender document could be written in less than a day.	Weak Candidate: As I did more of them, I got naturally quicker. I knew the answers and did not have to ask people for information.

Interviewer: *[Probing question to uncover feelings/motivations.]* Why did it feel to you that you didn't have much of a chance of success?

Candidate: This was a geography where local contacts are important. We did not have any track record of success and did not have any local contacts and partners.

Interviewer: *[Reflective question to understand basis for feeling or opinion, specifically if based on good reasoning and judgment.]* That's interesting to hear your views of that geography. Why did you feel this about this geography?

Strong Candidate: I had worked out there for three years in a previous company and observed that we landed contracts where we had good connections and wasted time and money on ones where we did not. We were selling the same solution in both situations.	Weak Candidate: Anyone who knows anything about that geography knows it is all about who you know. Interviewer: Do you have any direct experience working in that geography? Weak Candidate: Not direct, just general knowledge built up during my years working in sales.

Interviewer: *[Reflective question to explore sales competence and attitude in terms of tendering.]* What about tendering in general?

Strong Candidate: Personally, I think that tendering can be a real waste of time everywhere if you do not properly understand the landscape or have clear qualification criteria. I accept that in some areas it is unavoidable, but this does not mean that it makes good business sense to go after everything. I believe that you need to carefully track and manage the cost of acquisition when tendering or else you can really damage your business. You need to get very efficient at it.	Weak Candidate: Tendering is a fact of business in some sectors, and while it can take a lot of time and effort there simply is not another option. In most cases it is a numbers game. If you put in enough tenders, you will get something out. After all, statistically if there are four people in each tender, you are going to win 25% of them.

Interviewer: *[Probing to establish candidate's problem solving and creativity, and attitude to work.]* So, if this had been your decision what would you have done?

Strong Candidate: I would not have spent time and money tendering blind in that geography but instead spent time building some connections. It would have felt slower but probably got to a sale quicker.	Weak Candidate: Probably focused on a different geography. Interviewer: Tell me more. Weak Candidate: I don't think it is a good business plan to try to win in an area that you cannot get into. It is better to stick with selling where you can be successful.

Interviewer: *[Probing to establish candidate's approach to their manager.]* Did you tell your sales director that you did not agree with the approach to tendering in that geography?

Strong Candidate: I did talk to him about my concerns and shared my previous experience. I even suggested that we try building local contacts first, but he was clear that I should continue tendering regardless.	Weak Candidate: I probably said that I thought this was going to be difficult. Interviewer: Probably? Weak Candidate: Well, yes, I said something but it didn't change things.

Interviewer: *[Probing to understand motivation.]* How did that make you feel?

Strong Candidate: Frustrated, but I put my head down, made the process more efficient, and stuck with it. I also hooked up with some of my past contacts, and we eventually started to partner with a local firm and made some sales.	Weak Candidate: He was the kind of guy who always knew best so I just did what he said. Ultimately if he wanted to waste my time and the company's money, there was not that much I could do about it.

Interviewer: *[Summarising.]* Let me check my understanding. You questioned the instruction but ultimately carried it out...

In this example, the interviewer was looking for how the candidate dealt with being asked by their manager (authority) to do something they did not agree with. This was designed to give evidence of the presence or lack of the following:

- Confidence (willingness to question their manager, in an appropriate manner).
- Positive attitude and taking personal responsibility (how they attacked the task and also the request).
- Initiative (what they did to deal with the situation).
- Interpersonal effectiveness (how they responded to the manager's request).
- Effective communication (how they answered the question).
- Judgment (both how effective but also the basis for making judgments, i.e., facts and experience, or unsubstantiated opinion).

In the strong candidate, additional competencies were uncovered, namely strong efficiency orientation, goal focus, and prospecting behaviour.

Strong Candidate: Demonstrated positive attitude to work. Judgments based on facts and experience rather than opinions. Took initiative to reach out to contacts and creative approach to prospecting and business, thus solving their selling challenge. Good efficiency orientation and goal focus. Willing to challenge appropriately. Evidence of taking personal responsibility. Concise and informative style of answering questions.

Weak Candidate: Passive response evident. Judgments based more on personal opinion. Little evidence of creativity or business thinking. No initiative taken to improve or resolve selling challenge. Vague answers that required further probing. Evidence of not taking personal responsibility but leaving it with the manager.

Focused Listening

Whenever you are using behavioural interviewing, it is important to listen carefully to what is being said by the candidate. You need to be able to pick up on tonality and body language as well as the words used. Preparation is important here as well. If you are working out what question to ask next, you won't be able to listen properly to the answer to the question you just posed. Focused listening means exploring issues further when they don't feel right. For example, if a candidate says something hesitantly, you might want to say, "You sounded fairly hesitant when you said [x]. Can you tell me why?" Similarly, if the applicant uses "we" a lot, you will want to get clarity on what this particular candidate was responsible for and took the initiative to do on their own.

You will also want to think about your own tonality, body language, and words. If you fidget, look at your watch, and seem preoccupied, your candidate will naturally draw the conclusion that you are not interested or are bored. Sending such a message disrespects the candidate and damages the company's brand as well as your own. Even if you have concluded that there is not a match with this candidate, this person might well know someone you want to hire.

Examples of the Behavioural Interviewing Technique

Area	Traditional Interview	Behavioural Interview
Planning and organisation	Would you describe yourself as an organised person? How do you plan your work?	Tell me about a significant task that you had to complete by a specific and fixed deadline. What was the task and how did you go about it?
Resilience	Would you say that you are someone who keeps going when things get tough?	Tell me about a time when you cold-called someone and the person was really nasty and hung up on you. How did you feel? What did you do next?
Results Orientation Delivery	How do you ensure the success of a project that you are working on? How do you go about solving problems at work?	Projects rarely proceed without obstacles. Tell me about a recent project you worked on when you encountered a major obstacle. What did you do to get around that obstacle? We all face problems at work that are difficult to solve. Tell me about a problem that you were unable to solve on the first try. What did you do? [Listen for how the person varied the approach.]

Questioning Strategies

As you know, there are two basic types of questions—open and closed.

Open questions are effective for initiating a conversation, eliciting information, broadening the scope of the conversation, and, most importantly, keeping the candidate involved. Open questions may start with who, what, why, where, when, and how.

Closed questions tend to elicit "yes" or "no" answers, which are appropriate when you want the candidate to make a commitment, reach a conclusion, or make a decision. Closed questions may start with do, can, was, could, would, or has.

Some questions elicit intellectual or analytical answers. Others elicit emotional answers. "What do you think about making cold calls?" will likely elicit a different answer than, "How to you feel about making cold calls?" If you want to explore the candidate's thought process, ask thinking questions, i.e., "What do you think about...?" If you want to explore the candidate's reactions or emotional responses to a situation, ask feelings questions, i.e., "How do you feel about...?"

At its simplest, reversing is responding to a question with a question coupled with a softening statement (something that shows interest, gives support, etc.). Let's look at the following two scenarios that take place toward the end of an interview when the candidate is asking questions. Which ones gets you better information—where you answer the question or where you reverse?

Illustration 1 (Interviewer reversing):

Candidate: Do you require weekly call reports?

Interviewer: That's an interesting question. Why do you ask?

Candidate: In my previous position, they weren't required. If you hit your numbers every quarter, they left you alone.

Interviewer: I see. Was that a good thing or a bad thing?

Candidate: Personally, I like feedback. I know some people don't. But, I don't mind someone checking on my progress.

Interviewer: Interesting. Tell me about that.

Candidate: Well, sometimes it takes another set of eyes to help you see what's really going on.

Interviewer: Which means?

Candidate: Every once in a while, you can get caught up in an opportunity. Because there's a lot going on, you don't recognise that progress has slowed down, maybe even stalled. Another set of eyes can put things into the proper perspective and help you take the appropriate action sooner rather than later.

Illustration 1a (Interviewer answering the question):

Candidate: Do you require weekly call reports?

Interviewer: No, we don't.

Candidate: OK.

Illustration 1b (Interviewer answering the question):

Candidate: Do you require weekly call reports?

Interviewer: Yes, we do.

Candidate: OK. They were required in my previous position, too.

Illustration 2 (Interviewer Reversing):

Candidate: How much overnight travel is there likely to be?

Interviewer: That's a good question. You're asking because...?

Candidate: I did a lot in my previous position.

Interviewer: I understand. And when you say "a lot," you mean...?

Candidate: Ten to twelve days per month.

Interviewer: I see. And the consequence of that was...?

Candidate: Well, my family wasn't too pleased.

Interviewer: I can understand that. So if I were to tell you that you'd have to do a similar amount of travel in this position, what would you say?

Candidate: I'd say my family wouldn't be too happy.

Interviewer: I can imagine. Would it be fair to say that the amount of overnight travel the position requires could be a roadblock for you to accept the position if it were offered?

Candidate: It could.

Example 2a (Interviewer answering the question):

Candidate: How much overnight travel is there likely to be?

Interviewer: Typically, ten to twelve days per month.

Candidate: Oh, that's about the same as I'm doing now.

Watch out for non-specifics—"doubled sales," "grew by 40%," "top salesperson." Use follow-up questions to establish the real meaning. Top salesperson for one week in a team of two is quite different from top salesperson out of 50 for a whole year. When testing for the specifics, you should make a note so that you can ask for confirmation when checking their references.

More on Interview Questioning

When interviewing, you need to know what you are looking for. Often it is not the exact example the candidates pick that is important but what they do and why they do it. To help illustrate this I have included a number of different types of interview questions along with a marking score: what would be a positive indicator (+) and what would be a negative indicator (−). You can vary the questions and add some of your own, but take the time to think through your positive and negative indicators. Not only will this help you better evaluate the candidate, but it also takes out some of the emotion and unconscious bias ("This person likes football; I like football too," "Oh no, this person likes football; I think it's so boring."). Establishing a performance benchmark is also helpful when you are interviewing a number of people or when a number of people are involved in the interviewing.

General background questions

Question: What made you [the job candidate] decide that you wanted to be an xxx?
Marking:

(+) Well-thought-out reasons.
(+) Evidence of both rational and emotional factors.
(+) Understanding of options.
(−) Unable to articulate any reasons.
(−) Not in control of own destiny.

Variations: If you could start again would you have opted for a different degree, career, etc.?

Motivational questions

Motivational question: What do you like most about your current job? What do you like least?
Marking:

(+) Good self-understanding.
(+) Range of positives and gave examples to illustrate.
(+) Genuine example of managing the negatives.
(+) Enthusiastic about work.
(–) Sounded like they made up the negative to look good.
(–) Poor self-awareness.

Variations: What motivates you to go to work? What frustrates you? What makes you get up in the morning?

Motivational question: Why do you want to leave your current job/employer?
Marking:

(+) Well-thought-through reasons.
(+) Demonstrates commitment to current employer and intention to leave well.
(+) Honest.
(–) Sounds false.
(–) Divulged very significant issues with employer, colleagues, etc.

Variations: What would your current employer have to do to keep you? Why are you choosing to leave at this point in your career?

Capability questions

Capability questions: Give me an example of when you... Tell me about doing...

Marking:

(+) Wide range of capabilities.

(+) Evidence of successful delivery.

(+) Gave examples to illustrate.

(+) Genuine example of managing the negatives/learning from them.

(+) Examples of concern for impact, interpersonal sensitivity, leadership, and collaboration.

(–) Very narrow range of behaviours and influencing strategies.

(–) Poor structure (can be seen as poor analytical thinking).

(–) Vague and did not get to the point (can be seen as winging it).

Variations:

Focusing on past performance means questions like:

- Give me an example of when you had to solve a difficult problem.
- Tell me about a time you had to persuade someone to do something they did not want to do.
- Tell me about something that you have done to improve efficiency, reduce cost.
- Tell me about a time you felt strongly about something but your boss would not support you.
- Tell me about the worst decision you have made.
- Tell me about something you have done that you consider to be truly innovative.

STAR Model

The STAR model is useful as a prompt for behavioural interviewing. The goal is to identify the behavioural predispositions of candidates and their habits. It is about finding the facts about candidates' actual past performance and not making assumptions about what they might do or best guesses by them as to what they would do in a hypothetical situation.

The candidates should do the most talking. Keep focused on the information you need to acquire and keep on track. You need to orchestrate behavioural interviews very carefully, which is why it is important to always have two people—one to listen and ask questions and the other to listen and take notes. Like sales, don't ever have two people talk or ask questions at the same time. You can take turns from question to question or swap halfway, but for each segment only one person asks questions or talks. Look for evidence of skills, experience, attitudes, values and beliefs, results and learning, cognitive abilities, habits, and competencies.

- **Situation:** Here you ask candidates to describe (as a brief overview, ideally one sentence only) a recent challenge or situation. Use questions such as, "Tell me about...," "Give me an example of..." The key here is keeping it recent—ideally within the last 18 months. You are going to be asking for quite a bit of detail, and candidates need to be able to recall this accurately.
- **Task:** Here you need to determine what candidates wanted to achieve. What was the task? This starts to add detail to the situation.
- **Action:** This is the core section where you want to find out what the candidates were thinking, what they were doing, what other people were saying, and how they responded.

● **Results:** Here you want to find out what they achieved
and what they learned. Remember a positive result is not,
in itself, evidence of competence. Candidates might have
just been lucky, after all. Referring back to the philosophy
about Winners, the ability to fail and acknowledge that
failure and learn from it is a critical attribute of a Winner.

For the situation in STAR (or example in behavioural interviewing), personally I stick with work examples only. The problem
with non-work examples is that there are all sorts of dynamics
going on that do not apply or cannot be replicated at work. I
adopted the "work only" approach after asking a candidate to tell
me about something that he had achieved that he found personally challenging, and he used his recent wedding and struggles
with his future mother-in-law. This did not tell me what I needed
to know about his approach at work.

As I was getting close to graduating from college, I
went to a few assessment centres, a two-day selection
event with 15–20 graduates all competing for a few
jobs. In one that I remember, an assessor was really keen
on another (remarkably weak) candidate. On one occasion, he actually accused me of an action (not a good
one, needless to say) that this other person had done.
While a bit disconcerting at the time (luckily, I was
already sitting on a good job offer so not too distress-
ing), now many years later it gives me a great example of
unconscious bias.

Interview Guide

Putting together an interview guide is a useful way to keep things organised and to keep you on track in the interview. It also ensures that you are collecting enough data to be able to make a decision and refer back to in the decision phase. If you are interviewing a number of people, either on the same day or over a period of time, it is incredibly easy to get people and their answers mixed up.

These are the elements that should go into an interview guide.

Interview Guide
Position: Date
Candidate:
Interviewers (always have two) Interviewer 1:   Interviewer 2:
Preparation • Identify areas for exploration from their CV and covering letter. • Remind yourself of the role requirements. • Clarify your role and that of the second interviewer.
Outline for opening the interview Greet the applicant, giving your name and position and those of other interviewers involved. Go through a clear agenda—purpose, time, your role and that of your other interviewers, their chance to ask questions, and next steps. Explain the interview's purpose: • To acquaint interviewer and applicant. • To learn more about the applicant's background and experience. • To help the applicant understand the position and your company. • Describe the interview plan. • Briefly review past jobs/experience (key background review). • Ask questions to get specific information about skills, knowledge, and competencies. These will be pretty detailed to determine the fit for the role. • Answer questions about the position and organisation so the applicant can decide if the role is a fit. • Point out that you both will get information needed to make a good decision. Indicate that you will be taking notes. Make the transition to the key background review.

Key background review—clarification of experience	Notes:
Review application materials, including CV/resume and any application forms. Decide which jobs/experiences are most relevant to the target job. Prepare to conduct the key background review. • Note any jobs/experience on which you are unclear or would like more information (based on your SEARCH model). • Note any gaps in the CV. • Explore the applicant's experience and skills. **Possible additional questions for the applicant** If worked before: • "Take five minutes to briefly summarise your career to date referencing key decision points and relevance to this role." • "What were/are your major responsibilities/duties?" • "Have your duties and responsibilities changed; how and why?" • "What did/do you like best about the position? What did/do you like least?" • "Why did you (or why are you planning to) leave?" If not worked before: • "What made you choose your university and subject? Any regrets?" • "What has made you decide to pursue a career in sales?" • "Do you know anyone working in sales? Who? What does that person say about the job?"	

Behavioural qualities

This part of the interview is where you want to dig deep to discover the candidate's attitude, habits, behaviours, and competencies.

In preparation, you should have identified the six to eight aspects you wish to explore. These should link back to the role and your SEARCH model and be the same for each candidate. You should identify at least two possible questions for each. Sometimes the first question does not glean enough information so it is good to have a backup. It is important to ask the same questions of all your candidates. If you don't, you will not have a clear benchmark against which you can measure people.

To illustrate, here are some possible areas and questions to explore at this point of the interview.

Organisation and planning	• "Tell me about a significant task that you had to complete by a specific and fixed deadline. What was the task and how did you cope?" • "Can you talk me through a time when you have been under a lot of pressure to achieve your sales target or a piece of work? What did you do; how did you cope?"

Structure and process	• "How do you manage yourself to ensure you do not leave loose ends and keep on top of your pipeline?" • "Tell me about a time when you had to generate some data. What did you do to make sure it was accurate?" • "Tell me about a time when you lost or delayed a sale through not keeping on top of it."
Judgment and ethics	• "Give me an example when you were asked to do something that you didn't think was right. What did you do?" • "Can you share with me a time when you pulled out of a sale because the product was not right for the prospect or because you believed that the prospect was not going to buy and wasting a lot of your time?" • "Tell me about a time when you told a prospect or client that you could not allow them to do something, even if it was to your advantage, because it was not right for them."
Decisiveness	• "Tell me about a time when you had to make a rushed decision and it went wrong. What happened? What did you do to fix it?" • "We all have to make decisions every day at work. Tell me about one which you found particularly hard to make. Why was it hard for you? What happened?"
Tenacity, overcoming obstacles	• "We all face problems at work that are difficult to solve. Tell me about a problem that you were unable to solve on the first try. What did you do?" [Listen for how the candidate varied the approach.] • "Describe a situation in which your initial attempt to gain someone's support or cooperation failed. Did you try again? What approach did you use?" • "Give me an example when you dealt with a prospect who was very aggressive."
Achievement/results orientation	• "Tell me about a time when you achieved something that you found personally difficult." • "Tell me about something that you achieved in your role that you are most proud of." • "Tell me you top three personal goals. What were your personal goals last year, and how did you make progress toward them?"
Influence	• "Tell me about a time when you had to influence or persuade someone to do something that person did not want to do." • "Tell me about a situation where you managed to persuade someone to do something by first understanding that person's needs." • "What was some of the best ideas you have sold to your manager? What was your approach?"

Networking	• "How do you stay aware of the activities, priorities, and changes of other areas of your organisation? Why is this important? Give me a specific example of when you have done this." • "How do you go about developing good working relationships with people you do not meet with very frequently and have most contact with over the phone?"
Innovation and problem solving	• "Tell me about something you did at work that you consider to be truly innovative." • "Tell me about a time when a prospect or client wanted something that was not possible. What happened; what did you do?"
Communication	• "Tell me about a time when you had to communicate a difficult message to a prospect or client. What was it and how did you go about it?" • "Give me a recent example where you missed an important clue when talking with a prospect. What was the impact?"
Trustworthiness	• "Tell me about a time when a prospect was very untrusting of you. What did you do? Did you turn it around?" • "Tell me about the client who trusts you most. What did you do to gain that trust? What do you do as a result of that trust?"
Team orientation	• "Give me an example when you put the interests of the team above your own. Explain how." • "Tell me about a time when you were involved in team selling (or a team project). What was your role? What did you contribute to the team's effectiveness?"
Customer focus	• "Tell me about an important task/project/assignment you were working on for an internal customer for which the specifications changed significantly. What did you do? How did it affect you?" • "Tell me about a recent time when you have had to deal with an irate or unhappy customer."

Interview close	Notes:
Ask any additional questions. • "Are you interviewing anywhere else?" (Don't push for the company if the candidate is uncomfortable.) • "If we were to offer you the job, what would you do?" (Only if the candidate is a strong one.) • You might want to explore salary aspirations at this point as well (depending on the rest of your process). **Applicant's questions** Give applicant the opportunity to ask questions. (Note the questions asked here.) If time is tight, say: "We have xx minutes for your questions at this stage but you will have time to ask more questions later in the process." End the interview. Explain next steps in the selection process; don't over-commit on timescales and ask the candidate to flag any problems with the timescales. Thank applicant for productive interview.	

Interview Notes

Keeping quality notes is important in interviewing. It is likely that you will be interviewing more than one person. Without quality notes, candidates can start to merge into each other. You may lose clarity, which will damage decision making.

The following is an example of a notes template for a behavioural interview. There are more dimensions showing than you would normally be looking for in order to give you as detailed an example as possible.

	Rating	
Candidate Name:		
Position Applied for:		
Date:		
Organisation and planning The candidate organises and plans work; meets deadlines; increases pace and intensity if required.		
Structure and process The candidate has a clear sales template; sticks to the sales process; keeps the sale on track and moving forward.		
Judgment and ethics The candidate demonstrates good judgment and ethics.		
Decisiveness The candidate draws conclusions and chooses timely courses of action based on relevant facts, constraints, and probable consequences.		
Tenacity, overcoming obstacles The candidate demonstrates tenacity; finds different ways to overcome obstacles; tries and does what it takes to make the sale.		
Achievement/results orientation The candidate delivers on commitments; sets aspirational goals and works tenaciously to reach or exceed them.		
Influence The candidate effectively influences without pressure; can persuade managers and peers.		
Networking The candidate builds strong networks inside and outside the organisation; maintains contact to deepen relationships.		
Innovation and problem solving The candidate generates innovative solutions to the prospects' problems; tries different ways to deal with sales challenges.		
Communication The candidate clearly conveys information and ideas; encourages open and continuous communication; is keen to listen and learn.		
Trustworthiness The candidate develops and maintains trusted relationships with prospects and clients; establishes parity and equal business stature.		

Team orientation The candidate collaborates effectively across team boundaries; refers and gains referrals from colleagues; achieves but not at the expense of colleagues.		
Customer focus The candidate focuses actions on customer needs; develops and sustains strong customer relationships; effectively handles customer problems; does not over commit to gain a sale.		

Interview Summary Sheet

This form should be a single summary of the full interview programme following discussions at the interview wrap-up session. It will avoid the need for interviewers to retain their own copies of any interview notes and will enable Human Resources to respond to requests for feedback.

Date of Interview(s):	
Position:	
Interviewers:	
Points to Note: • Please ensure that you feel comfortable with all the comments you write. • The comments should be brief but please ensure that they are sufficient to enable the reader to identify why the decisions were made; e.g., do not simply say "technically not very good" but endeavour to identify areas where technical competence was not as required. • Please use examples from the interview wherever possible. • Be careful not to make cross-comparisons between candidates in the record of the notes—the comments should be on their own merits. • Try for a balance of positive comments as well as areas for improvement. • Please attach a copy of your interview questions and the interview programme to this sheet. • Remember that in some situations these notes may be disclosable to candidates.	

Candidate Name	
Technical Interview	

Personal/behavioural interview	
Presentation	
Psychometrics	
Decision/outcome	
When all interviewers are satisfied with the comments above, please shred all original interview notes and return this document to HR for filing.	

Candidate Evaluation Form

The easiest way to manage the evaluation process is to keep a candidate checklist for each candidate. Here you should record core information on your candidates as they work their way through your selection process.

Candidate Name:		
Position Applied For:		
Interviewers:		
Date:		
CV Screening		
Experience/Capabilities	Rating	Comments/Evidence
Qualifications How well do the candidate's academic and professional qualifications fit the job needs?		
Career history, experience, and achievements What aspects of events and achievements in the candidate's career history and experience are especially relevant to the job needs?		
CV Screening Decision	Rating	Rationale:
Psychometric		
Test 1 outcome		
Test 2 outcome		
Psychometric screening decision	Rating	Rationale:
Telephone Interview		
Interviewer		Date
Strengths		
Areas of concern		
Topics to raise at face-to-face interview		
Telephone screening decision	Rating	Rationale:

Reference Interview		
Areas of strengths		
Areas of concern		
Reference conversation decision	Rating	Rationale:
Face-to-Face Interview		
Behavioural strengths		
Behavioural weaknesses		
Are these weaknesses trainable?		
How important are the areas of weakness to the job?		
Interview	Rating	Rationale:
Overall assessment and recommendation		

Rating Scale:
1 = Inadequate for the job in question
2 = Adequate for the job in question
3 = Good fit for the job in question
4 = Superior fit for the job in question and may have further potential
5 = Outstanding fit for the job in question and has further potential

Decision Code:
P = Progress to next step
A = Appoint
B = Hold as backup
C = Consider for another role. Use comment box to make suggestions.
R = Reject

Chapter Summary

This chapter has explored the qualifying and selecting steps of the hiring model. Key messages include:

- Design your qualifying and selecting step in line with the role you are hiring.
- Use a range of inventorying tools: CV, assessment tests, references, interviews, exercises, and social media.
- Think about how you can use assessment tests to increase the quality of your decisions as well as improve your qualifying.
- Think about qualifying as a screening funnel where you are taking steps to reduce the number of potential candidates down until you are in a position to make a final selection.
- Pre-plan your interview questions to increase consistency and consider in advance positive and negative indicators.
- Use behavioural interviewing rather than more traditional type interviewing.
- Make appropriate interview notes and use these in the decision-making process.

CHAPTER 7

Appoint and Onboard

This chapter looks at the appointing and onboarding of your successful candidate.

The appointment process includes deciding on to whom to offer the position. This should be done based on facts collected during the process, which will allow you to determine the level of fit to the job you have specified, and should incorporate input from multiple internal sources.

Once you have reached a decision, you will need to follow a well-designed approach to making the job offer.

This chapter also covers post-appointment communication and onboarding, often overlooked factors that are critical to employee success, motivation, and retention.

Deciding

Since all participants in the interview process need to give input into the final decision, the best practice is to bring all those involved in the selection process together in one meeting to make the decision. This ensures that all views are collected and the necessary discussion can take place. Decision-making meetings need to be held as soon as practical following the conclusion of the interview process while memories are still fresh. The purpose of a meeting is to arrive at a decision; i.e., offer a candidate the position, reject all candidates if unsuitable, re-advertise, or arrange second interviews.

Participants in the meeting can use the candidate summary sheet as the basis for their decision. Actual examples of behaviour should be used when recording highs and lows of each candidate against the selection criteria. A key output from the meeting will be to agree on next steps—who is going to inform the candidates of what information, including whether to provide feedback.

The recruiting manager is responsible for informing successful candidates of the terms of their offer. For applicants who are new to your company, it is important to state that the offer is subject to medical examination (if this is your policy), favourable references, and proof of right to work in the country.

Following verbal confirmation of acceptance, all other candidates will be rejected. For internal candidates, the best practice is for the recruiting manager to tell the candidate's current manager, who will then have a discussion with the candidate. You can then confirm the decision in writing. For external candidates, you should use a standard rejection letter.

Several factors may prevent interviewers from assessing a candidate objectively.

- **Stereotyping.** This is personal shorthand that fits people into categories based on a single or small number of characteristics and then projects the remaining characteristics in that stereotype onto them.

- **Halo/horns effect.** This is the tendency to see only good or only bad things from candidates regardless of their actual performance because the interviewer has decided in advance how candidates will perform. This is particularly likely if candidates remind you of someone—a child, partner, sibling, or friend.

- **Self-image.** This is the tendency to see candidates that are like yourself in a favourable light. This can be particularly unproductive as differences are valuable in increasing creativity.

- **Comparative not criteria-based judgment.** This is when you compare the candidate not to the criteria you have determined necessary but to other people, other candidates, the previous job holder, or even yourself.

- **First impressions (primacy effect).** This is making a judgment about candidates very early in the interview and allowing that to affect your view of the rest of the candidates' performance.

- **Recency effect.** This is allowing the most recent or final impression to have a dominant impact on your judgment of the candidate. You need to use notes to avoid this.

- **Central tendency.** This is the tendency to avoid extremes in ranking the performance of candidates on the interviews. It makes it extremely difficult to come to a final decision.

It is important to be aware of these issues. Ask yourself when forming an opinion about a candidate: "What data am I basing

this on? Is my interpretation of this data affecting my view of it?"
The use of several interviewers in the process also helps guard
against the problems above, since they will each have a different perspective.

For the decision meeting:

- Record highs and lows from the interview.
- Classify them against criteria in the job/person
  specifications.
- Consider strengths and weaknesses of the candidates.
- Weight each according to importance to the job and
  trainability.
- Consider essential characteristics before desirable
  characteristics.
- Consider trainability of skills and the candidates' ability
  to learn.
- Make and keep notes on reasons for decisions.
- Collate interview notes.

Offering

The offer is classic negotiation, and therefore negotiation best
practices come into play.

With any negotiation, it is important to get your candidate to
speak first. Ask them what their aspirations for salary and total
compensation are. Where this is legal and in line with your company's policies, advise the candidate before you ask them this
question that it is company policy to validate this information, so
you will be looking at contracts and pay stubs and/or conducting
a credit check.

If you are going to verify past salary levels, I suggest you tell
the applicant this before you ask for current compensation

Remember that many candidates only compare base salaries so you need to ensure that the total compensation is understood by both parties. This includes salary, benefits, bonus and commission, training and development, and other key aspects of the employee value proposition.

information. While it may be tempting to see if you can catch them out, you probably do not want to trick a candidate into becoming unhireable due to a little embellishment in the heat of the moment.

Once candidates have given their expectations, you should state yours. If the gap between your offer and their aspiration (as opposed to current actual) is very large, you might want to share your fear that this role or your company might not be a good fit.

There are two main schools of thought on where you should start with your offer. One school would advise that you decide your final position up front but make a low offer—say 80% or 90% of your position. Then you hitch up once to 95% and hang in for as long as you can. If that does not work, you can then "go to a higher authority" before making the final offer, which would be the 100% point.

It can work. However, I don't really like it. It feels a bit too similar to discounting in a sale. It destroys trust. You are effectively giving the message that if you "bargain," you can improve your salary. This is a bad habit to train into your new hires since it is likely it will carry on throughout their career. This can manifest in them regularly threatening to resign to take up a better offer unless you counter it—not a brilliant way to manage your people. You are saying, "My word is not my bond."

If you adopt the alternative approach, which is, "My first offer is my final offer," especially for senior executives and salespeople, you need to position it correctly. You need to tell the candidate your strategy and the fact that you don't reverse discount; otherwise, they may think they are playing a different game. You also need to get the information from them in advance so you can properly think through your offer before making it. Clearly if you have missed something that comes out in the discussion, you might have to reconsider and discuss, but this would not be the strategy with which you set out.

When negotiating salary, you need to be careful to avoid defending and justifying your position. Your candidate does not want to hear that you would love to pay them more but have to worry about internal realities. Believe me, I was told this once

> In one of my corporate roles, we used to hire people from an industry sector that paid better than we did, at least short term. We had a few things on our side: we were smaller and had much broader roles with more variety; in some roles we offered long-term wealth (stock, value share, etc.). For these roles, we wanted risk takers. I would say very clearly at the interview, "If you are focused on salary, we will not be the right move for you. While we can match your current salary, we will not compete in a bidding war with your current employer. If you are looking for an opportunity for wealth creation, with some risk, we are going to be a good fit."

and I was unimpressed. Your tonality when positioning an offer is important. If you sound tentative, your candidates may hear this and go in for the kill. Take responsibility for your offer, position it well, and let them decide.

Internal and External Communication about the Hire

Remembering your employee value proposition, the communication process needs to be as well managed as the hiring.

A strong communication step includes the following:

- **A drafted internal announcement ready to go out on Day 1.** Generally, I would recommend an announcement on their first day at work and not in advance. It keeps things fresh in other colleagues' minds. You should include the following in the announcement:
  - Name of new hire, job title, department, and date of joining.
  - Brief description of previous employment and role, if appropriate.
  - A little bit about them as a person—ask them to give you a quick sketch—and include a picture.
  - Description of the new starter's job and responsibilities.
  - Welcome to the new hire and well wishes in the new role.
  - Include any message of thanks to former jobholder if appropriate.

  Note: For executive roles it will also be appropriate to make an external announcement. This should be drafted in advance ready for dissemination on the start date. With executive appointments, it might be appropriate to send the external announcement out a bit in advance depending on the situation. If this is the case, the internal announcement needs to be made at the same time.

- **A well-managed interval between the date of offer and the start date.** For some roles, this can be quite a long period. You need to maintain contact with your new hire during this period and start the bonding with your company and colleagues. Consider options such as inviting the new hire to any company social events, if their appointment is known to the team prior to this event. Informal announcements at such an event are fine and do not remove the need for the more formal appointment announcement on Day 1. Also, put some information together that you can send about the company. Clearly if the hire is currently working for a competitor, this should not be commercially sensitive information. However, general information would be fine. As it happens, this also helps mitigate against a no-show.
- **Preparing the space.** Planning for Day 1 and onboarding should take place during the interval as well as sorting out the logistics—desk, chair, equipment, etc.

Onboarding

Onboarding is a critical part of your hiring process. A well-structured onboarding process can dramatically shorten the time to effectiveness. This benefits not just productivity and results (for salespeople, it will impact top-line numbers), but it also increases motivation and engagement of the new hire. People like to be successful and need to feel they're doing well as quickly as possible in a new role. Poor or non-existent onboarding can also result in lower retention and early loss of talent.

It's a huge waste of time and money to hire qualified people only to have them leave after a few months because they feel undervalued, confused, let down, or are not performing as well as they would like. All of these problems can be prevented with a decent onboarding programme.

Feedback is important to all employees, and the sooner you start this the better. I recommend that you give feedback to new hires or promoted staff, telling them exactly why you selected them but also advising them of the areas of concern the selection process highlighted. This feedback should include their assessment test results. The outcome of the session should be a clear development plan that covers both areas of strength and areas for development. This session should also be used to outline the expected deliverables for the first six or twelve months. This will give your new hires a clear sense of purpose and control—they know what is expected and what they will be focusing on.

For internal promotions, this can be immediately after they have been notified of their promotion. You should have a strong enough trust relationship to do this immediately at the point of highest impact. For those new to the organisation, this should happen during the first week but not the first day (it will be a bit too overwhelming) and ideally not the end of the week when they might feel that they wanted to know earlier.

Let's turn now to the onboarding process.

Purpose of onboarding:

- Helps staff become effective.
- Reduces disruption and maintains safety.
- Ensures new hire feels valued and is integrated quickly.

Content of an onboarding programme:

- Site familiarisation.
- Safety and security procedures.
- Meeting relevant contacts.
- Determining accountabilities and objectives for first year.
- Determining training and development needs.
- Schedule for learning key aspects of the role.

Responsibility for undertaking onboarding can be given to the new hire, but the accountability remains with the manager.

The best practice is to provide individuals with an onboarding pack (electronic is fine) with all the key information they need, including links to company sources. Create a list of the information that new hires will need to learn and also the people they need to meet. Many times, they can set up the meetings themselves, but you should have alerted your colleagues to the need to meet your new hires.

Regular reviews should be scheduled in. You must not forget the more social side of things—arrange for colleagues to go for lunch with new hires during their first week.

The first day and the first week are critical to establishing your new hires. Try to achieve a balance whereby they get to do things on their own but are not simply told to sit at their computer and read a bunch of documents. If reading and assimilating lots of data is critical to their role, give them some exercises to complete. This will keep things more interesting and also enable you to test understanding and progress. For example, if you want them to learn about a client, ask them to put together a short summary of five insights into the client and share these with you.

My recommendation is that you schedule Week 1 on an hourly basis and then have goals in place for Weeks 2 and 3 that can be reviewed on a daily basis. Giving your new hires responsibility for monitoring their own progress not only takes the burden from you but also increases their engagement and ownership.

Make sure that they adopt the necessary work disciplines from Day 1. When hiring salespeople, this means that you need to get them on the phones within the first week. Indeed, this is true when you hire any people who have a lot of phone work to do in their jobs. If they cannot start to contact prospects without some additional knowledge, you can find something meaningful and useful for which they can get on the phones.

Creating a checklist covering what new hires should know and be able to do or deliver during their induction programme and using a RAG status approach is a great way to track progress. RAG status is giving a red, amber (yellow in the United States), or green to denote progress. In this situation red would mean not started, amber would mean started but ongoing, and green would mean mastered.

Area of Activity	Desired Outcome	Target Completion Date	RAG Status
Set up on computer, with appropriate access and passwords	Able to access company systems including CRM	Morning of Monday Week 1	G
CRM	Able to find information	Tuesday Week 1	A
CRM	Able to input data	Wednesday Week 1	A
CRM	Able to generate call lists	Thursday Week 1	R
Accountability	Initial work plan developed	Thursday Week 1	R
Messaging	Able to make convincing 30-second commercial	Friday Week 1	R
Calling	Confident at answering inbound calls	Friday Week 1	R

Knowledge	Knows top three products and able to give short description of each	End Week 1	G
CRM	Able to create reports	Friday Week 2	R
Calling	Able to qualify inbound calls	Friday Week 2	R
Calling	Confident at making outbound calls to clients	Friday Week 2	R
Accountability	Consistently update work plan daily for three weeks	Friday Week 4	R

Day 1

Ensure there is a desk, chair, phone, computing equipment, and stationery ready on Day 1 for your new hires. Even if you have formal orientation, safety briefings, etc., the new hire's manager should be there to greet them when they arrive and also bring them around to say "hello" to their coworkers before being taken off for formal onboarding. If you do not do this, they will sit in reception and then be taken to a room and told about safety, company policies, IT protocols, etc., and it will be lunch time before they meet any of the people with whom they are going to be working. It feels cold and boring, which is not the impression you want to give on Day 1. These elements are critical, but can be done second. If there is something they need to know before walking around your premises, their manager can always tell them.

Example of First Week Schedule

	Monday	Tuesday	Wednesday	Thursday	Friday
8:00–9:00		Arrive and settle in	Arrive and settle in	Arrive and settle in	Arrive and settle in
9:00–10:00	Arrive 9:30 and meet team	CRM 2: Elizabeth	Overview of Products 3: John	Client Orientation: Alex	Go with Adam on client visit
10:00–11:00	Safety, IT, and HR Briefing	Work time: CRM practice	Work time: Produce product presentation	Intro to inbound calls	
11:00–12:00		Overview of Products 2: Alex		Observe and start taking inbound call (supervision by Chrissi)	Work time: Taking inbound calls (with support)
12:00–1:00	Intro to CRM: Elizabeth	One-to-one hiring feedback session	Observe John calling		
1:00–2:00	Lunch with new team	Lunch with Adam	Lunch with Elizabeth	Lunch with Team	Lunch with other new hires only
2:00–3:00	Work time: CRM Exercises	Introduction to work plan, followed by work time: Create own work plan	Work time: Prepare and practice 30-second commercial	More on CRM: Elizabeth	Make product presentation
3:00–4:00				Work time: Creating call lists from CRM	Work time: Taking inbound calls
4:00–5:00	Overview of Products 1: Adam	Meeting with Marketing team	Meeting with Finance team	Coaching session: Listen to recorded inbound calls	Review of week, prepare for review meeting, give 30-second commercial
5:00–5:30	Review with Manager	Review of day and personal learning log	Review of day and personal learning log	Review of day and personal learning log	Review with Manager

Performance Evaluation

As detailed in Chapter 2, the cost of poor hires is very high and becomes higher the longer they remain. You therefore need to include in your onboarding process early performance evaluation and feedback processes. Catching something early and giving feedback gives your new employee a chance to correct and change. They may be doing something that they have previously been told to do that does not fit with your company. You want your new hire to develop positive habits early in the role and to avoid forming bad habits. To this end, you need to ensure that they immediately start key aspects of the role. Phone calls are a good example of this. If the role is going to include making a number of dials on a daily basis, they need to be on the phone on Day 1; this will have a direct impact on their subsequent phoning behaviour. For many roles, it will not be appropriate for them to be calling prospects or clients on Day 1, but you should find some phone work for them to do—list updating, information gathering, etc.

Additionally, you need to think about some early indicators that are a cause for concern and will tell you quickly if the candidate is going to succeed. If you have not thought these through in advance you will be much slower to pick up on these.

To illustrate, for any role, you need to establish on Day 1 (and reinforce this) the core daily behaviours. For a sales role, an example would be that they need to make 50 dials a day. If they are not consistently doing this in Weeks 2 and 3, they are not going to be successful, and you need to address this immediately.

Chapter Summary

In this chapter, we have explored the appointing and onboarding phases of hiring. Some key messages include:

- Adopt a systematic approach to the decision-making process, benchmarking each candidate against the required criteria, ideally at a group meeting with everyone involved in the selection process present at the same time.
- Focus on behaviours, what the person said and did, and not impressions, to avoid unconscious stereotyping.
- Establish the strategy for the offer phase, in particular your response to any push-back or negotiation by the candidate.
- Plan for announcements of the new hire.
- Design and implement a formal onboarding programme. A quality onboarding process will be a positive experience for your new hire (or internal appointee) and lead to quicker time to effectiveness, greater motivation, improved retention, and higher performance.
- Start performance evaluation and feedback immediately.

CHAPTER 8

Measure and Improve

easurement is critical to any process. When it comes to hiring, however, it is often overlooked or only short-term lag indicators are measured.

Process improvement is only possible if you measure and track performance. Measuring is all about ensuring that you have a process that is efficient, effective, and fit for its purpose.

Measuring effectiveness is about looking at the output or result of your process. It is evaluating how consistently you are able to create a quality pool to select from and how competent you are in selecting top performers for your roles.

In short, you need to be sure you are measuring two elements of hiring: the inputs—process and behaviours—and the outputs—number and quality of hires.

The third area to measure is your personal selection competence. As we've said before about recruitment overall, spotting talent is also both a science and an art, and you need to focus your development in both these areas. The science part is building competence to deploy effective selection tools (psychometrics, interviewing, behavioural interviewing, and assessment centre assessing). The art side is about honing your intuition, your feel, and your judgment. To do this, you need to make notes of what your feelings were and the judgments you made. Reviewing these in the light of new and additional evidence about your candidates after they have been working for you for a period of time will enable you to build your competence in this area as well.

I have worked with a lot of managers and business owners. Some are simply brilliant, naturally so. A bit like maverick salespeople, they are to be respected but not emulated. Others are just awful. They are often top performers themselves but just cannot spot talent. These are also not to be copied. The ones I recommend as worth learning from are those who have systematically built capability and developed themselves into highly effective recruiters who make decisions based on evidence and sound judgment.

Measurement

Develop a set of metrics, which might include:

- Cost per hire includes all the costs involved from the time the recruitment process commences until the selected candidates are fully effective in their role.
- Time to hire (also referred to as speed of hire) refers to the time from when the position fell vacant to the time a replacement is found and begins work. Reducing time to hire has the obvious benefit of reducing costs (the more efficient your process is the less costly it is), but interestingly it also improves your quality of hire as well. Strong

candidates do not stay in the market for long so if you drag your candidates through a long, drawn-out process, you will most probably lose the best ones.

● Satisfaction should be measured, both of the requester for the new employee as well as the new recruit. Develop a recording system for both of these aspects.

● Quality of hire means measuring the ongoing quality of the recruit.

● Retention means to track the retention of hires.

● Evaluate the sources of hiring, both from the point of view of which sources provide the greatest volume of applicants but more importantly which provide the highest quality candidates, along with from which source the selected candidates came. This information should drive subsequent decisions on where to invest for future recruitment. This is an important measurement since people frequently have preconceptions about sources of hires and need to evaluate these so that they are making strong, consistent sourcing investments.

● New hire satisfaction means seeking feedback from new hires (at 30 days and 90 days). This is critical to assessing the efficacy of your recruitment. New hires should be asked about their hiring experience (process, communication) as well as their onboarding process and how closely the job matches their expectations. A mismatch in expectations needs to be addressed immediately by the manager but should also be used to improve the recruitment process. Expectation mismatches may lead to low productivity and expensive resignations just at the point you would expect the candidate to become effective.

● Offers to acceptances ratio is important to track, along with reasons given for not accepting a role.

- Interviews per hire should be measured in order to not needlessly waste time (and costs). Keep the number of candidate interviews down to a sensible number. Skilled pre-selection (including telephone interviewing) should mean that this should be around three and certainly no more than four per hire. If you are hiring multiple people, you can push this ratio down a bit, so if you are hiring four people you should aim to interview, say, nine candidates rather than sixteen. If you find yourself interviewing too many people for a role, you should probably have a look at the effectiveness of your screening process.

- Candidates per hire is another useful metric. It can give you information both on the effectiveness of your recruitment message as well as your sources. You are aiming for a reasonable number of on-target applications. Too few, and you may not be reaching the A-Players; too many, and you will spend a lot of time screening.

By tracking information about the recruitment process, you can identify opportunities for efficiencies, reducing or controlling costs, and improving quality.

If you use online sources for candidate attraction you should consider the following measurements:

- Getting found: number of unique users and candidate registrations.
- User conversion: number of applications.
- Candidate conversion: ratio of applications to short listing to placement.
- Candidate engagement: returning visits, response to job alerts.
- Candidate attraction: followers, retweets, refer a friend applications.

● Social reach: range of social platforms that candidates come from, depth of engagement on different platforms.

A Balanced Scorecard Approach

Measuring your recruitment effectiveness is critical to streamlining your process and ensuring quality recruitment at the right price. No single measurement (for example, cost of hire) should be taken in isolation, and some are more within your control than others. It is therefore beneficial to take a broader approach to reviewing performance. The following suggests four areas that should be measured.

Candidate Perception	
Measures candidates' satisfaction with their recruitment experience	
Metrics	Example
• Quality • Responsiveness • Transparency • Honesty	• Satisfaction with the recruitment process • Satisfaction with the interview experience • Satisfaction with Day 1 and onboarding experience • Surprises with company or role after joining • Feedback on Glassdoor
Process	
• A formal check-in with new hires should take place in the middle of their first week (to cover the recruitment process, interview experience, Day 1, and onboarding plan). Generally this should be conducted by: someone who was not the interviewing manager; HR if you have someone who does this; or perhaps their buddy if you have a buddy system for new hires. • At the end of the first month, another check-in should be scheduled. This should be with their manager. Here you want to look at how they are doing with their onboarding, their colleagues, and their new role. A very useful question to ask at this point is what surprised them on joining (with job, company, etc.). This enables them to share any disconnects they may have experienced (so you can work through them) and also provides feedback to the company about this that are out of line with the statements made during the hiring process.	

Performance
Examines cost and effectiveness of recruitment

Metrics	Example
• Work-in-progress cost per hire • ROI of different sources (direct, agency, referral, etc.)	• Number of vacancies being handled • Cost of different sources and number of high quality candidates from each source

Process

• Cost per hire is one of the core recruitment KPIs you should track in recruitment. It is a quantitative measurement.
• Talent sourcing should be managed the same way you would any marketing activity. You need to have clear goals, performance metrics, and a budget. You should evaluate the different channels for efficacy and ROI. This is an ongoing activity with an annual review and budget-setting process.
• Tracking fixed costs and variable costs is also useful.

Process Effectiveness and Efficiency	
Examines how well specific activities are tracking against agreed performance standards	
Metrics	**Example**
• Time to hire • Interviews per hire • Candidates per vacancy	• Actual time to hire vs. target • Ratios of interviews to hiring (lower is better)

Process

• These metrics should be part of your core recruitment KPIs.
• Tracking performance against target gives you a benchmark.
• It is helpful to benchmark your performance against competitors and best in class companies.

Quality	
Measures the quality of the hiring outcomes	
Metrics	**Example**
• Quality of candidates • Retention of candidates	• Ratio between shortlisted candidates and job offers • Candidate retention • Three-month performance evaluation • Three-year review to track performance and potential (have they been promoted, are they a high performer?)

Process

• Measuring and evaluating quality (see section below).
• Candidate retention should also be tracked as part of normal business KPIs. If you track candidate sources, you can use this to evaluate your sources as well. For example, you might find that candidates with a certain background just don't stay, in which case you need to figure out if this is fixable or if you need to avoid that source.

Quality of Hires

Measuring the quality of your hire warrants a bit more exploration. It is probably the area of least measurement yet one of the most relevant. One reason so few companies measure this is that it is not easy (time to hire requires little more than three columns in a spreadsheet—date started the hiring, date new hire accepts the job, and a column to calculate the lapsed days) and the other is that it needs to be tracked over time.

Let's break it down into four timeframes.

1. Immediate actions upon hiring

At the point of hiring, make a note of candidates' potential in your view in terms of where they might get within the organisation within their first five years.

At the same time, make a note of what you think they will be achieving in terms of job performance. Regarding salespeople, what sales do you think they will make in their first three months, six months, twelve months, as well as Year 2 and Year 3? Track actual performance against this. Often once someone is hired, other priorities take precedence and performance isn't evaluated as closely as it should be. The lack of a benchmark makes it hard to evaluate.

Even when you have clear performance benchmarks for the salespeople, it is a useful exercise to see if you have correctly anticipated their performance. If you consistently overestimate or underestimate, this is something to consider. Is it because your targets are incorrect or because you are not yet effectively spotting talent when recruiting? The individuals' success will naturally depend on their performance, but your success as a recruiter will depend on your ability to accurately predict future performance of your hires. Write it down at the point of hire, and then, of course, check back at regular intervals.

Write down three areas that you feel your new hires will excel in and three where you think they need development. Evaluate this against reality as evidenced over the new hires' first three to six months. This too will help you hone your recruitment and predicting skills.

One final measure at the point of offer is to rank the hires against your current talent and others you interviewed. This will tell you if you are consistently hiring A-Players and if the A-Players to whom you make offers are accepting your offers.

2. Between three and six months after hiring

Measure output compared to other new hires and where you would expect them to be. In sales recruitment, this is fairly easy to do since you can simply measure sales output. It is also useful to evaluate and compare their sales work plan and ratios.

The manager's assessment of performance and behaviour is as important as output at this early stage. You can also measure knowledge of your products and market.

3. Twelve months after hiring

After a year, you can measure:

- Behaviours
- Outputs and results
- Customer feedback, complaints, or satisfaction
- Co-worker feedback

It is important when evaluating salespeople's performance to consider their impact on the whole sales process and customer experience. If salespeople set up their relationships badly by overpromising or giving away free stuff during the sale, this will have an impact further down the line with account managers or customer service teams. It is important to evaluate these tendencies. Thereafter you should deploy normal performance management to help develop your new hire to be the best that they can be.

4. At three and five years after hiring

Review how they are progressing in line with your predictions at the point of hiring. This is a good way for you to hone your skills in terms of predicting longer term potential. It also gives you information about the effectiveness of your training and development.

Chapter Summary

This chapter talks about measuring, learning, and improving. These are critical if frequently overlooked steps within the hiring process. Here are the key messages.

- You will want to measure:
  - The process itself—is it timely, consistent, and efficient?
  - The effectiveness—does it bring you the desired results, i.e., talent?
  - Your selection competence—are your judgments accurate?
  - Impact on candidates and potential future hires.
- Use a balanced scorecard approach. No single measure should be taken in isolation.
- Measure the quality of your hires at different timeframes (immediate, short term, and longer term).

CHAPTER 9

Working with
Recruitment Agencies

I have included a chapter on working with recruitment agencies because they warrant a bit of attention, in addition to the comments in the "Partnering" section in Chapter 5. I am defining a recruitment agency as a company that sources candidates—finds and pre-qualifies talent and gives them to you to evaluate and make a hiring decision.

My opinion is that while recruitment agencies have a part to play in a recruitment strategy, if you are going to use them, you need to invest in the relationship and work in partnership toward shared goals. The way that you work with your recruitment agency will impact the quality of service and candidates you receive.

Your first step to success is to have a clear idea of how working with recruitment agencies fits your overall hiring strategy. This will underpin your relationship. Do you want to maintain a transactional relationship or a partnership? Both are possible, but there are implications to your choice.

In this chapter I propose to first outline briefly the three main types of contracts, to explore the type of relationship you can have—transactional or partnership—then touch on preferred supplier lists, and finally look at measurement.

When to Consider Using an Agency

The following provides some ideas on when working with an agency can be useful.

- **If you can better focus on core business.** For some businesses, it makes sense to focus on the core business. This yields a far higher margin than the cost of using an agency, and thus it makes commercial and business sense to keep managers focused on the business and not overly distracted by the sourcing of talent. If you are a high-margin business, measure how much time and attention is being spent on hiring activities that could be provided by an agency. Then work out the relative costs and benefits of using an agency to source and prequalify all your hiring. You cannot, of course, avoid time and investment on your employee value proposition and creating an environment in which talent flourishes and remains.

- **If you have low levels of hiring.** If you typically do not hire many people in a year, it can also make good commercial sense to let experts do this for you. They will have greater reach and already have partially, if not fully, mapped the talent in the market. The time and money you would need to invest to be able to compete in the scramble to find and attract top talent is not likely to be warranted by the amount of hiring you are doing. Paying fees to agencies will be an overall cost saving and at the same time give you access to better talent.

- **If you are looking for scarce skills.** Here you may go for a blended approach, keeping core recruitment in-house while using an agency to track down scarce skills for you. This is particularly relevant if most of the people with the skills you want work for a direct competitor since you do not want to be approaching them too obviously (it is "bad form" but more importantly may open the floodgates to their head hunting all your top talent). Additionally, these people most probably will not be actively looking to change jobs. Agencies can better attract them away from their current roles and facilitate them considering yours. If you want to leave finding talent to outside agencies as your sourcing strategy, you might benefit from having more than one agency on board: individual niche agencies to track down candidates with scarce skills and a more general one for your other vacancies.

- **If you are a small company.** You may well already be covered under the low levels of hiring but even if you are trying to do a lot of hiring to support a fast-growth opportunity or strategy, you may struggle to compete effectively for top talent in the marketplace. Using an agency may get you access to top talent that might not initially approach or consider you as an employer, but on learning more about you and your story and ambitions, may find you an attractive proposition. Agencies can get you past the first barrier (knowing) and potentially help you with the other barriers to attracting Winners.

- **If you are struggling to fill a role or roles.** Pragmatically, if you have not filled a role in the timeframe you have set (remember to have hiring timeframes in place up front) you may consider using an agency. The cost of holding a vacancy open for longer may be more than the cost of agency fees.
- **If you want to access some or all of the benefits of using a third party.** These are some of the benefits you can receive from recruitment agencies:

  - Knowledge of the marketplace, allowing them to advise on role design, salaries, etc., to best position you as a hiring company.
  - Ability to access talent that is not currently in the market.
  - Broader talent pool giving you access to more talent (including less obvious sources and talent in non-related fields).
  - Higher levels of trust at the outset. If an agency is really good (and surely these are the only ones you should work with), they can quickly gain trust of candidates and facilitate their exploring the option of working with you (i.e., getting over the initial hurdle).
  - Independent negotiation of fees, etc., which then don't colour your working relationship once the individual starts.
  - More time to search, resulting in a faster hire.
  - Better ROI than doing it in-house.

Clearly, all of these benefits can be achieved using in-house resources. It will only make sense to use an agency if you choose to not do this in-house or if it will result in untenable direct and opportunity costs.

When considering whether or not to work with a recruitment agency, it is useful to do a cost/benefit analysis. Calculate the rough costs of your undertaking the search in-house (direct costs, opportunity costs, and likelihood of success) and then look at the fees. For salespeople in particular, they can both be hard to find and expensive to look for when you take into account lost sales (opportunity costs) associated with the search process. You cannot avoid time spent on selecting, onboarding, or ensuring the right work environment, leadership, and management, and you therefore might be better off focussing on this rather than the search part. Equally, this may be a core part of your business success, in which case invest wisely in building in-house competence (supplemented if appropriate with outside help).

Types of Agency Contracts

Broadly there are three main types of contract arrangements, namely:

- **Retained.** This is when you agree on a fee (typically in the 25–33% range) with a single agency and they undertake a full search for you—you put them on retainer. Payments are made in three stages: at the point of starting (30% or one third), at the point you are provided a shortlist (30% or one third), and at the point of offer (40% or one third). If you walk away from the arrangement, you forfeit fees paid. Typically, this arrangement is in place for senior hires when they have to be tracked down and lured away from their current company. You are heavily invested in the agency's success and give them all the help you can.

- **Contingency.** This is where you brief an agency on your job but only pay them if you make an offer to a candidate that they put forward. There is no commitment on your part to not search for the candidate yourself at the same time or to not offer the same brief to more than one agency. In terms of money, you are not taking any risk (thus the willingness to use more than one agency). You are, however, taking a hidden risk in terms of the speed to hire and the quality of the talent pool that will be offered to you. I am not saying that agencies deliberately short-change clients who procure them on a basic contingency basis, but I also believe that we need to be reasonable here. When it's your own clients, which ones get the red-carpet treatment? The ones who have worked with you for years and have been loyal, or the ones that chop and change between you and your competitors on a job-to-job basis, based on the latest quote? I am sure they both get your excellent service levels, but might you just go the extra mile for the former?

- **Contingency with exclusivity.** Here you still only pay on results, but you agree that you will give the agency exclusivity. This means that you will not place the job with other agencies. The benefit here is that you still have the control of paying on results only but you can forge a strong partnership with the agency and ensure that you are getting their full commitment and attention. You can limit exclusivity to three weeks or six weeks or twelve weeks (whatever is reasonable for the hire that you are making). In fact, contingency with a time limit is a sort of bonus scheme and can reap rewards in terms of performance (many people work better with a deadline).

Transactional Relationship

As implied by the description, this is working with the agency or agencies on a job-by-job basis and keeping things fairly transactional. Underpinning this approach is the philosophy that agencies are a commodity business and should be treated as such.

As a buyer, you will always find an agency who will agree to work on a transactional basis and agree to your fees. You need to ask yourself if this is what you want.

The likely behaviours you will exhibit include:

- **Using multiple agencies on a contingency basis.** The idea here is that more people working for you is better. They carry the risk of investing time and not making a placement.
- **Pushing down on fees.** If your underpinning belief when working with agencies is that their product is a commodity (one agency is much the same as another and one candidate is much the same as well), then it makes sense to pay as little as you can for it.
- **Low interaction.** Toss a brief over the fence and then keep low and avoid calls from the agency, telling them to email candidates over to you. Why waste time talking to them? You can simply read the CV.

The likely implications include:

- Extra work for yourself since agencies on a contingency basis will generally want to get as many candidates over the line to you as quickly as possible to keep out the competition, who are all working to place the same role.
- A possible bias (perhaps unconscious and highly unlikely to be formally stated within the agency) to keep the better

candidates for better clients when they know that they will be better appreciated and paid well.

- A lower level of understanding of your company and culture resulting in less effective matching (you might have to interview a few more or take a few goes to get them to fully understand the subtleties of the brief).

Partnership

As the name implies, this is a relationship based on win-win. Both sides get their needs met. As the buyer, you can decide that this needs to be a relationship where this happens. It does not mean rolling over on the fees and paying more than you are comfortable with, but it does mean that you are committed to a longer-term relationship and if your expectations are met you will remain a loyal customer. You can still work a contingency model in a partnership, but my preference is to offer a limited-period exclusivity (with contingency) because this drives better performance by the agency.

The likely behaviours you will exhibit include:

- Accept responsibility for the relationship and invest the time and energy to ensure that that agency understands the company, culture, and all the needs of the role.
- Be willing to take advice; they are, after all the recruitment experts. For example, if they say that you need to reconsider the search parameters if you are going to find the candidates you want, you will do so.
- Agree to a reasonable fee and balance this against the benefits of a swift, high-quality placement (which is the reason you are engaging the agency in the first place).

One thing to consider is whether to agree to a fixed fee rather than a percentage. Do this openly and agree mutually on the likely salary for the new hire. I always did this when working with agencies, and it worked well. My motivation was not to squeeze them on fees (I took their advice on market salaries for my role) but so that if, in the end, we had to go up on salary to secure a particular candidate, the line managers (I was VP Global HR) did not get grumpy about the fee (which could sometimes get in the way of a pragmatic approach to salary). When agreeing to a fixed fee, if the decision is taken to change the brief midway and offer a much higher salary to reflect changed accountabilities, I would expect a hiring manager to initiate a re-fixing of the fee—as all partners would.

The likely implications include:

- A clear, mutual understanding of each other's roles, commitments, and obligations.
- Access to better agencies—after all, the strongest agencies might turn down the transactional, pure contingency, low-fee model.
- A stronger relationship with a faster placement and better candidate matching (saving you time and effort).
- Less noise (fewer agencies in play).
- Strong, signed-off performance standards and KPIs (it is important that you both set and evaluate these).
- Regular conversations when working on finding a candidate.
- Regular conversations to manage the partnering relationship.

One area to note is around fees. Recruitment agencies define the compensation on which you will be paying the percentage differently. At one end, it is just starting base salary; at the other end, it could be the total money paid to the hires in the first year. Take care before you sign a contract to know what you are signing. You do not want to be paying a percentage of any relocation costs or even the signing bonus.

Preferred Supplier Lists

It would be impossible to write a chapter on agencies and not talk about preferred supplier lists (PSLs). These were introduced to reduce the chaos that can happen in recruitment when you get as many agencies working on jobs as you have line managers. The idea is that you work with a limited number of agencies covering different areas of your recruitment needs. This protects your line managers from repeated calls or speculative candidates.

Ideally PSLs are a form of the partnering model. They can work well provided you have selected your agencies carefully and have good conversations with them about performance, etc. Where they don't work is when the PSL agency cannot find you the candidate that you are looking for and the manager coping with the vacancy is not getting the support they need. You need to maintain control. If the PSL agencies are not performing on a particular vacancy, you might want to give another agency a try, having first discussed this with your PSL agency or agencies.

If you have or wish to have a PSL, consider the following:

- Have a mix of small, niche agencies and larger ones (they come with different benefits and compete less directly with each other).
- Try to avoid a feeding frenzy across your PSL agencies. Don't just throw your jobs over the fence to all of them but select according to the vacancy and their particular skills.
- Don't feel that you need to pay all PSL agencies the same.
- Ensure that you manage your agencies with clear performance standards and KPIs, collecting feedback from

recruitment managers and the candidates themselves as part of their evaluation.

- Ensure all hiring managers are with the programme and not undermining it with side deals (recruitment agencies can be quite persuasive). Have a process whereby managers can seek to introduce an agency to the PSL if they have very special requirements (but control this or else you won't have a PSL).

Fees

Different agencies charge different fees. This is a mature market, which means that generally, but not always, the fees correlate with their quality. I would not advocate pushing fees down on principle but at the same time would not advocate over paying. Test the robustness of their fees. If they consistently charge at this level and are still in business, chances are that they are earning their money and you will be paying a fair rate. If you feel that they are gaming you, push back (gently and politely, of course). If they start high and drop quickly, this raises a red flag that you should explore further.

If you achieve a low fee deal and there is not a good business rationale, I would be concerned about the amount of attention your role will be given and the quality of the candidates. Once again, talk this through.

One of my clients told me a story of an agency that they were talking to about a new sales role. The agency told them that they had two fees. The higher fee included extra support with defining the role and psychometrics. My client was getting this support from me so felt no need for it. He therefore elected for the lower rate. This would have been fine had the agency not added that those people on the higher fee, naturally, also got the better candidates. I would not work with an agency like that for any fee.

Thus my advice to pay the right fee for the right candidate; it needs to make commercial sense for both parties.

Performance Measurement

Setting and agreeing to performance standards with your recruitment agency is critical. Using a balanced scorecard approach, as outlined below, works well.

Candidate Perception	
Measures candidates' satisfaction with their recruitment agency	
Metrics	Example
• Quality • Responsiveness • Understanding	• Satisfaction with the recruitment process • Satisfaction with the interview experience • Satisfaction with the agency's understanding of the company and the role
Process	
• As part of the Week 1 check with candidates, you should include a review of their experience with the recruitment agency, including their credibility, their capability, and the quality and responsiveness of their service. • The candidate's satisfaction with the agency's understanding of the company and the role should form part of this check.	

Customer Perception	
Measures the company's satisfaction with the agency's services	
Metrics	Example
• Quality of service • Responsiveness • Communication	• Satisfaction with agency service • Satisfaction with agency responsiveness • Frequency and timing of updates
Process	
• Managers and HR should take time to review their experiences with the agency via monthly, quarterly, or annual reviews, which are built into the contract with the agency. • Setting and agreeing to performance standards with your recruitment agency is critical.	

Work-in-Progress	
Examines how well specific activities are tracking against agreed performance standards	
Metrics	Example
• Time to hire • Candidates per vacancy • Change control • Volume	• Actual time to hire vs. target • Numbers of qualified candidates put forward for a vacancy • Monitor any time the brief is changed • Number of vacancies being handled
Process	
• These metrics should be part of your core agency KPIs. • Tracking the agency's performance against target gives you a benchmark for performance.	

Quality	
Measures the quality of the hiring outcomes	
Metrics	Example
• Quality of candidates • Match of candidates to the brief	• Satisfaction with quality and suitability (how closely they match the brief) of candidates • Ratio between candidates recommended by the agency and job offers • Candidate retention • Three-month performance evaluation • Three-year review to track performance and potential (have they been promoted, are they a high performer?)
Process	
• Measuring and evaluating the quality of candidates put forward should form part of your review with the agency.	

Chapter Summary

This chapter has been all about working with recruitment agencies. Key messages include:

- Working with a recruitment agency can make sense. The option should be evaluated as part of your recruitment strategy.
- The following situations lend themselves to working with recruitment agencies: benefits from focusing on the core business; low levels of hiring, seeking scarce skills, small company; unknown brand, struggling to fill a role.
- Agency contracts broadly fall into three types: retained, contingency, and contingency with exclusivity.
- You will get greater benefits from building a partnership than keeping the relationship transactional.
- Setting and agreeing to performance standards with your recruitment agency is critical; using a balanced scorecard approach works well.

CHAPTER 10

The Recruitment Evolution

As has hopefully been shown in this book, it's important to move from reactive to strategic recruitment. This move is an evolution and cannot be done overnight. To further explain this evolution, we will examine the key elements of each of these stages.

Phase 1: Reactive

This is the stage where everyone starts. The duration you remain in this stage depends on your ambition and belief: your ambition to grow your company and your belief that your key differentiator is always going to be your people.

Key aspects of the reactive recruitment phase include:

- Vacancies are unanticipated.
- New hires are recruited to fill the immediate vacancy with little to no long-term view.
- There is no managed recruitment budget (you find the money if and as required).
- Employee productivity and morale is impacted by recruitment delays.
- Projects and important but less urgent development activities are delayed when there are staff shortages.
- High reliance on external agencies is required to source top quality and specialist candidates.
- There is little to no control over which agencies are used; tactical not strategic relationships are built with agencies.
- There is high but unmeasured cost of bad hires (wrong person, leave within first six months, etc.).
- Managers see recruitment as a chore.

Phase 2: Operational Focus

This phase starts to see systematisation and process improvement. The focus is on the recruitment operation and making this as effective as possible. It is an essential stepping stone to strategic recruitment; if your operations are not optimised, you will waste time and money if you try to be more strategic.

Key aspects of the operational focus phase include:

- Effort, time, and money is invested in recruitment process mapping and improvement.
- There is strong focus on costs and operational efficiency and numerous efforts to reduce/contain costs.
- There is some attempt to manage recruitment across the

organisation but 100% compliance is rare. This is seen as an administrative control, not a strategic business imperative.

- There is the emergence of preferred supplier lists and approved recruiters but little measurement of effectiveness; the focus is more on cost control.
- Decentralised recruitment budget is developed.
- HR role is still focused on policing the system; HR and line roles are blurred.
- There is low compliance with company policy (especially regarding use of agencies).
- Performance metrics are weak or absent (or at best limited to cost and efficiency).
- There is little focus on employer brand and building a competitive employment value proposition.
- Some workforce/succession planning is in place but the continued focus is on vacancy filling.

Phase 3: Strategic Focus

This phase is where recruitment is seen as a strategic business imperative. The value placed on quality recruitment is greater than vacancy filling. Taking the long-term view reduces the stop/start rhythm of the earlier phases and smooths out the impact of individuals leaving the company.

Key aspects of the strategic focus phase include:

- There is a strong strategic focus.
- Short-term requirements balance with longer term strategic considerations.
- There is a centralised recruitment budget.
- A measurement culture is established with clear metrics and continuous improvement.

- More than process is measured—and value add is included.
- The HR role is clearly seen as adding value; HR and line roles clear.
- Line managers give 100% compliance based on a full understanding of the policy and its beneficial impact.
- There is an established partnership with one external recruiting partner, possibly augmented by one or two specialists on a similar partnership basis.
- There is a clear, congruent employer brand with a compelling and competitive employment value proposition.
- Talent management processes are fully aligned with business strategy and direction.

Chapter Summary

The focus of this book is moving from reactive to strategic recruitment. This concept applies equally to small and large companies, although the details will, naturally, vary. This should be a journey, an evolution, that moves from purely reactive to more operational and finally to strategic.

EPILOGUE

Building capability in hiring is critical to the long-term success of any company. There are a number of building blocks that contribute to capability development in an organisation.

Strategic Framework		
• Where is the company going? Its overall purpose, ambitions, and strategy. • How is hiring positioned within this? Strong and congruent employee value proposition.		
People	Processes	Tools/Technology
• Managers trained and competent • Partners, strategic alliances, agencies in place • Current employees mobilised—talent scouting, alumni engagement, buddy systems	• End-to-end resourcing process in place • Focus on forward planning and strategic recruitment as well as tactical vacancy filling • Agency election and management (if appropriate)	• Recruitment tools • Career portal • Media/social media
Management Information and Learning		
Consistent measurement, key metrics, lag and lead indicators		
Communication		
Managers, workforce, applicants, alumni, talent pools		

There is a lot of information in this book, with lots of ideas and suggestions. You cannot possibly tackle everything at once—and you don't need to. My suggestion is to review your current process and effectiveness, pick one or two things to change that you feel will give you the best return, and take it from there. Make it your goal to keep improving the process over time. That is what strategic recruitment is all about.

Look for these other books
on shop.sandler.com: